Exodus for Ordinary People

Exodus for Ordinary People

Unwrapping the Second Book of the Bible

By Paul Poulton

RESOURCE *Publications* · Eugene, Oregon

Resource Publications
An Imprint of Wipf and Stock Publishers
199 W. 8th Ave., Suite 3
Eugene, OR 97401

www.wipfandstock.com

PAPERBACK ISBN: 978-1-4982-8892-7
HARDCOVER ISBN: 978-1-4982-8894-1
EBOOK ISBN: 978-1-4982-8893-4

Manufactured in the U.S.A.   AUGUST 3, 2016

Dedicated to Rev'd David Brian Poulton
"Out of Egypt I called my son." Hosea 11:1

Contents

Contents

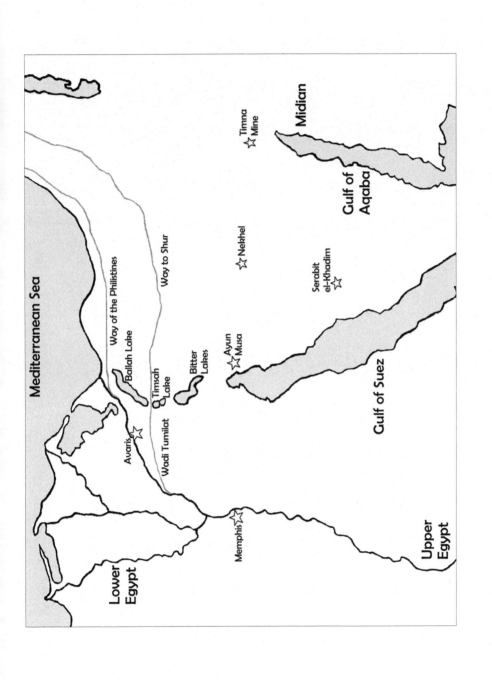

Chapter 1

Two Lights

THE BOOK OF GENESIS informs us about the seed that was planted in the human race: the seed that was first placed in Adam and made its way eventually to Jesus—The promised seed. In the book of Genesis the safekeeping of the seed with all its attendant adventures takes us all the way to the fledgling tribe of Judah. And there we must leave it, for the time being, because the second book in the Bible takes us on a different route: the book of Exodus directs our gaze towards the children of Levi.

Levi, the man, had not showered himself with glory: in his anger he and his brother, Simeon, butchered the men of Shechem and hamstrung their oxen. Their father, Jacob, was ashamed of his sons' behavior, and predicted that their offspring would be scattered in Israel. Once in the "promised land" the tribe of Simeon lived in the area that had been allocated to Judah, and the numbers in his tribe dwindled. The Levites were assigned no land at all; however, they were allowed to live in cities within land that had been allocated to the other tribes of Israel. Jacob's prophecy hit the mark.

The change of subject matter between the books of Genesis and Exodus is pertinent to the bigger picture. Judah (in Genesis) and Levi (in Exodus) have been picked out for us to view. It's as if the Bible is saying, "Watch this!"

When I was a youth and part of a "youth group" a "youth leader" would sometimes show us a movie. At the end of the movie an adult would sometimes offer an explanation of what the movie was all about and point out several spiritually relevant themes. As teenagers we always seemed a little restless once the movie had finished and didn't really want to be

1

"talked to" about the whole thing again. It was as if the adults didn't think the movie had quite done its job and needed some help to convey its message. That doesn't happen in Genesis or Exodus, we get the message, "Look at this," and that's it. No summing up, no closing remarks, no epilogue. The movie we are watching in the early books of the Bible is strong enough to convey its own message by the story alone. All we have to do is read it and the story will do its own work in our hearts.

Stories are brought before us in Genesis and Exodus to look at and listen to, and as we contemplate them we realize they are alive with ideas. In the New Testament we are told that the word of God is living and active, and this seems to be true. The story of Judah is shown to us because the genealogical route to Christ was running through his line. And now in Exodus we are presented with Levi because his children are chosen to liaise with Yahweh and thereby support their fellow countrymen in understanding who the Lord is. In this way they will get to know Yahweh's personality, learn what he wants, and what he can do for them (and us) if we befriend him.

In Genesis chapter 1 we read that God made two lights to shine, a "greater light" and a "lesser light." The theme of the "bright light" and "not-so-bright light" resonates with the greater light that appeared on the banks of the Jordan River, of which the lesser light said, "He must increase, but I must decrease" (John 3:30 nasb). Later we are told that Jesus is the light of the world (John 8:12) and John the Baptist is also called a light (John 5:35). Jesus descended from the tribe of Judah, and John the Baptist descended from the tribe of Levi. Although John was born before Jesus, in truth, Jesus came before John, similar to Genesis coming before Exodus. John the Baptist, as his Levitical heritage dictated, told the Israelites what God required from them. He also prepared the way for the Lord, and when John saw Jesus walking nearby he told the people to "Watch" or "Behold" because here was the Lamb of God.

When Jesus was transfigured on the mountain, Moses and Elijah appeared with him. Moses was from the tribe of Levi and Elijah is compared to John the Baptist who is also from the tribe of Levi (Matt 17:12–13). Jesus, as we stated, was in a genealogical line embedded in the tribe of Judah. The books of Genesis and Exodus take their parts as players in the great drama: Judah and Levi leading us forward.

Chapter 2

The 400-Year Prediction

WHEN YAHWEH AND ABRAM agreed on a contract, Abram was told that his descendants would be strangers, or, as the Septuagint says, "sojourners," in a country not their own for 400 years (Gen 15:13). Isaac's birth was the starting point for this period. Isaac was born in Canaan but the country didn't belong to him or to his father, in fact Abram himself was still considered a relative "newcomer" to the area—a Hebrew, one of the Mesopotamians who had "crossed over" the Euphrates. The British Museum links the name Hebrew with *Habiru*, a name assigned to people (in ancient writings) with no specific homeland, who have journeyed and lived a nomadic existence on the margins of society. The *Habiru* were known all around the Fertile Crescent, from Sumer in southern Mesopotamia all the way to Egypt. Abram certainly fits the bill: he had journeyed a long way and lived in tents, as the aptly-named book of Hebrews says, "Abraham, when called to go to a place he would later receive as his inheritance, obeyed and went, even though he did not know where he was going" (Heb 11:8). He was a *Habiru* who became known as the famous Hebrew. Abraham's son Isaac was also a stranger in Canaan, and his posterity were strangers and sojourners in Paddan Aram and later in Egypt.

Yahweh had told Abram that in the fourth generation his descendants would return to Canaan (Gen 15:16), which means the four generations begins with Jacob because his father, Isaac, never left Canaan, but Jacob died in Egypt. We can see this highlighted with Moses's family tree. The first generating was Jacob fathering Levi, the second was Levi fathering Kohath, the third

3

was Kohath fathering Amram, and the fourth was Amram begetting Moses who led the people back towards Canaan in what is known as the exodus.

Isaac's birth as the starting point for Yahweh's 400-year prophecy was an important feature of Jewish history. We know this because Paul, in Acts 13:16–20, points his fellow Israelites and some Gentiles to the 450-year period that ended when the Israelites' conquest of the land of Canaan was complete. Paul started his calculation from when Isaac was born, which is fairly easy for us to work out. There were 430 years from Abram's promise to when the law was given to Moses (Gal 3:16–17). Caleb said he was 40 years old when the first group of spies went to survey the land, which happened around 2 years after the law being given to Moses. If we add 2 to 430 we get 432. Caleb also states that he was 85 years old when he asked for the mountain as his part of the inheritance of the land towards the end of the conquest. That's 45 years for Caleb, which we need to add to the 432, giving us 477 years from when the promise was first given to Abram. Then we need to add the time it took Caleb to remove the Anakites from the mountain before the land had rest from war, which wouldn't be too long, probably about 2 or 3 years, taking us to 480 years. Now we need to take away 30 years, because Abram was 70 when he received his first promise and 100 when Isaac was born. So if we take 30 away from 480 we are left with Paul's 450 years. Paul himself calls the number an approximation, but it's precise enough to see the starting point is taken from Isaac's birth.

According to these calculations Israel first became a land-occupying nation in 1356 BC (400 years from Isaac's birth to the exodus as told by Yahweh to Abram, plus 40 years wanderings, and 10 years until the promised land was free from war). This would give the nation of Israel 150 years to become a recognizable nation in the eyes of the surrounding countries as recorded by the Egyptian King Merneptah on a stele that was recovered and is dated around 1207 BC.

At this point we ought to take note that some people are extremely skeptical about the book of Exodus. Some modern scholars tell us that the book of Exodus was put together sometime between 500 and 600 BC with final revisions taking place in the post-exilic 5th century BC. But if Moses was the book's writer then it must have been written earlier, as the exodus itself took place in 1406 BC and Moses only lived another 40 years after that. According to some teachers the book of Exodus was redacted, and made to look as though it was written concurrently with the events that take place within its pages.

Part of the problem is that modern books written about history require some verification of sources, and books of the Bible that claim to report historical events involving God are not always accepted as historical because some people do not accept God as a cause of events, so the books are not considered factually historical. This happens not only with historical books of the Bible but also with books that claim to be prophetic. Take the book of Daniel for instance: the book prophesies about Media and Persia and Greece becoming dominant political powers, which is what actually happened. If you are happy to accept that God's Spirit does speak prophetically through people then you can also accept that Daniel could have written the book. But if you think that prophecy does not occur then the date the book of Daniel was written could be placed later than the events it describes.

The skepticism of some scholars has a way of infiltrating society as a whole. This may be verified by a photo caption I recently saw on a popular newspaper website about the movie *Exodus: Gods and Kings*. The caption said,

Christian Bale plays fictional religious character Moses in Exodus.[1]

There are two ways of reading that caption: Moses *is* a fictional entity, or the *version* of Moses that Christian Bale portrays is fictional. I hope the second interpretation is the correct one, but there are people who will go for the first option.

To help alleviate some of this skepticism we may be able to verify the dates in and around the exodus from a different frame of reference. If we take 1406 BC as the year of the exodus and 1356 BC as the time that Israel finally had rest from war (50 years—40 years wanderings and 10 years until the promised land was free from war) we can assume that the general population of Israelites had begun to settle, but Caleb still had a few battles to take on. Then, as Joshua 14:15 states, "the land had rest from war." The ploughing, sowing, and general cultivation of crops would probably have started while Caleb was still finishing his battles on his mountain. So we can take the preceding year, 1357 BC, as an approximate year the general population of Israel began to cultivate the land. Moses had told the Israelites to note when they started to sow crops and count off 49 years, and then on the 10th day of the 7th month of that 49th year a jubilee year would start. The jubilee years also confirm the dates we are looking at. Every 49th year—seven sevens, as stipulated in Leviticus 25:8–13—was considered a

1. Malm, "If Moses Lived Today," photo caption.

jubilee year from when the Israelites were able to plough and sow fields in Canaan. So the counting of the jubilees started in 1357 BC.

Ezekiel starts his book by telling us he received his first vision in the 30th year. Ezekiel is good with marking time so he doesn't mean the 30th year of captivity, because when he uses the captivity as a date marker he states it. The 30th year Ezekiel refers to is probably the 49 years of jubilee. The nation of Israel was in the 30th year of its current jubilee cycle. He also lets us know that Jehoiachin was in his 5th year of captivity. Historians say Jehoiachin was taken into captivity in 597 BC, so the 5th year of his captivity would be 592 BC. Ezekiel told us that the same year was the 30th (of the jubilee cycle) so if we add 30 to 592 we get the year 622 BC as the beginning of the jubilee period that Ezekiel is talking about. If we then add 15 cycles of 49 years (735 years) we arrive at the year 1357 BC, which points us to when Israel first became a land-cultivating nation.

Chapter 3

Big Ark Little Ark

THE STORY ABOUT THE birth of Moses in the book of Exodus, and his subsequent voyage in a basket made of reeds, is reported by some sources to be borrowed from an earlier account of a Mesopotamian king whose name is Sargon. The "Legend of Sargon" is written in cuneiform and was discovered at Nineveh in 1867 AD. King Sargon reigned in Mesopotamia from 2270 to 2215 BC and according to the inscription, Sargon's mother was a high priestess who gave birth to him in secret and placed him in a basket constructed of reeds made watertight by applying bitumen to the tiny vessel. She then launched the reed basket into the river Euphrates to be taken by the gods where it will. Aqqi, a man who lived further downstream, spotted the abandoned mini-boat with its precious cargo and rescued the craft and its contents from the flowing waters. Over the next few years Aqqi raised Sargon as his adopted son. Sargon went on to make quite a name for himself, and became a man of the people. He was open about his humble beginnings and the people took him to heart and he rose to become the founder of the famous Akkadian Empire.

So that's Sargon. The parallels with Moses's infancy are easy to see. The skeptical response is that the writer of Exodus heard the story of Sargon and superimposed an Israelite version of events on the original legend. In a court of law it would be easy to see how the biblical defense team would proceed:

"I put it to you ladies and gentlemen of the jury, if one such baby has been put into a river and left to float on the arbitrary currents of the waterway, does that stop another baby being treated in a similar manner? No, it does not! In fact ladies and gentlemen of the jury, would it not make it more likely that if a baby had been placed onto a flowing river and successfully retrieved once, that other mothers wishing to hide the fact that they had been pregnant would do a similar thing?"

And the defense team would have an excellent point. In fact Sargon's mother was not the first to place precious infantile cargo afloat in a craft. The news of the great deluge, which Bible readers know as the Flood had reverberated around the whole Fertile Crescent, everyone was aware of the devastating Mesopotamian flood. And what made the story of the Flood so compelling was Noah and his family's escape in the ark. The story was covered extensively in the press of the day, the reading material of which was clay tablets rather than paper. Each tablet had names for the hero applicable to their own area: "Atra-Hasis" in the Akkadian press, "Ziusudra" to the Sumerians, "Utnapishtim" to the author of the book *The Epic of Gilgamesh*, and "Noah" to the writer of Genesis. Each name or title meant something to each group of people who were intended to read it, but it seems fairly certain they were all the same person.

Believers in the Bible, of whom I am one, take the Flood account as preserved for us in the book of Genesis as the main reporting of the event, but that is not to say the other accounts have nothing to offer us. One of the main themes running through the Mesopotamian accounts of the deluge is the god Enki (Ea to the Akkadians) speaking to the hero of the story through a reed wall. The reed wall is a part of the hero's house. Enki is on the outside of the house and the listener is on the inside. The reason this whispering through a reed wall is going on is that Enki is about to relay a secret message that he only wants the recipient he's singled out to hear. The first part of Enki's communication informs his hearer that he ought to spurn his house and build a boat. Furthermore he is told not to worry about his property but to remember that saving life is what counts. Houses in ancient Sumer were sometimes made of sundried brick and other times made of reeds. In fact reed houses can still be seen in southern Iraq today, built in much the same way as they were all those years ago. The reeds grow very tall indeed and weaving and plaiting them is a skill that the Mesopotamians secured for themselves early on in their history. The reed houses they made were strong, with stanchions placed at intervals to maintain the integrity of the structure and give strength to the arching roofs. There are photos of these very large reed houses that can be seen by a quick search on the Internet and one of the first things we notice about them is how similar they are to the hull of a large boat. They look like pictures of the ark that we have seen, but placed upside down.

At the ancient town of Hit (situated near the river Euphrates, about 90 miles northeast of Baghdad) there is a bitumen spring and, as reported by archaeologist J. P. Peters in 1888 AD, a boatyard. The boats that were built at the boatyard were traditional Euphrates rivercraft looking remarkably similar in rectangular shape to the ark described in Genesis. J. P. Peters took photos of the reed constructed boats and the caption to the photos begins, "A Noachian Boatyard . . ."[1] Another visitor to the boatyard in the 1800s was Lt. Col. Francis Chesney who was sent to the area to compile a government survey. When Lt. Col. Chesney saw these reed boats he was struck with the irresistible thought that these boats could be similar to the boat made by Noah. Chesney wrote a detailed report of how these boats were constructed using branches every 8 to 12 inches interwoven by a basket work of reeds. Hot bitumen is then used to coat all the surfaces, making the boat fit for its purpose. Chesney pointed out that a similar boat could be built having dimensions described in Genesis using the same basic framework, and without too much trouble. He addressed some skeptics of Noah's ark in his day by remarking that "objections raised on account of the supposed difficulty of the work, may be considered as obviated."[2]

A boat made of reeds sounds to us like it might be a bit flimsy, but these boats are far from fragile. In an ancient "Ark Tablet" that was recently discovered and is now on display in the British Museum, Atra-Hasis tells us he set up 3,600 stanchions for the framework of the boat. Worthy of mention at this point is that 3,600 is what the Sumerians called a *sar*, and a sar was sometimes used to indicate a big number. Irving Finkel, who is an Assyriologist at the British Museum, explains that although sar means 3,600 the Mesopotamians could use it to mean any number that is large. For instance today we use the word "myriad" to mean any number that is massive, although strictly speaking myriad means 10,000. The Sumerians might say, "may the moon god keep you well for a sar (3,600 years)," which means may you enjoy good health for a long time. Or we may say, "I looked up at the night-time sky and saw myriads of stars." Both examples mean "many." So when Atra-Hasis tells us he used 3,600 stanchions for the boat he was building, it could be another way of saying that no one going on

1. Peters, *Nippur or Explorations*, 163.
2. Chesney, *Expedition*, 639.

board this vessel needs to worry for their safety because the framework is extensive and strong.

Bundles of reeds were tightly packed and interwoven around the framework for the outer shell of the boat, and then of course, a thick coating of bitumen was applied. Many reed-impressed pieces of bitumen are among the archaeological finds in and around Iraq. They date back to earlier than 5000 BC. The boats constructed by the Mesopotamians were strong and seaworthy. Examples of Mesopotamian reed-impressed bitumen with ancient barnacles still attached have been found around many parts the Persian Gulf coastline. Also found around the gulf is pottery that the Ubaid people who lived in lower Mesopotamia around 5000 BC were famous for.[3] The boats the Mesopotamians made were structurally sound and even used on the sea for maritime trade.

Slabs of bitumen with reed impressions on them have also been found in northern Iraq and surrounding countries. Let's remember that Berosus reported that in his day (290 BC) Noah's massive boat could still be seen at its resting place on the mountain of the Cordyaeans and that people were breaking off pieces of the hardened bitumen and taking them home as souvenirs. Some of the reed-impressed bitumen that now sits in museums could be from Noah's ark.

The plaiting of the reed work and palm-fiber rope used for the body of a Mesopotamian boat was sturdy and used in antiquity for transporting goods and human cargo along the wide rivers. Atra-Hasis also explains that the caulking of his boat was not done sparingly either, pointing out that it was one finger thick. He adds that a final coating of lard was applied on top of the bitumen, which was also one finger thick.

The Bible informs us that the ark was made from gopher wood, but no one knows for sure what gopher wood actually is. Many attempts have been made to identify the word "gopher," and different versions of the Bible make an attempt at its identification. Dr. Fritz Hommel, who was a professor of Semitic languages, identified "gopher" with the Assyrian word *giparu*, the word used by Assyrians for "reed."

Let us suppose that Noah's ark was made in the normal way Mesopotamian shipwrights built their vessels. The deluge was a major event for the people groups who lived in or around the area and the story of a man building a boat and saving lives was passed on from generation to generation. I explained in the book *Genesis for Ordinary People* that in and around the

3. Carter, "Neolithic Origins," paras. 1–2.

Fertile Crescent during the early days of human civilization, babies were sometimes given up for adoption. Although the method used to declare that a baby was "up for adoption" did sometimes mean the baby had first to be abandoned and if someone happened to find the baby, then documentation could be acquired for the finder to become the legal parent or guardian of the baby. The hit and miss method of giving up babies for adoption may have been alleviated by the story of Noah. The word for "ark" in the Old Testament is only used for two scenarios—once for Noah's boat and once for the boat that baby Moses was placed in. We know that Moses's boat was made from reeds, and there's reasonable information to suppose that Noah also used the tall and tough Mesopotamian reed for his boat. The craft that Moses floated in was a lot smaller than Noah's ark and the type of Egyptian reed was different too. The word for the reed used describing the boat that held Moses is *gome*. The word used for Noah's Mesopotamian reed appears to be "gopher." Both boats were waterproofed in much the same way. It looks at first sight that Noah had set some sort of precedent. King Sargon's mother, for her own reasons, kept her pregnancy a secret. She abandoned her child to the fate of the gods, and made a model of the famous boat that saved Atra-Hasis, or Ziusudra, or Utnapishtim, or of course, as we know him, Noah, for the purpose of giving baby Sargon a fighting chance.

Setting a baby afloat on the river Euphrates in a well-made replica of the ark would be a far better option than what had formerly been used to abandon babies in what is described as "to the dogs," because if a baby were abandoned in an open field or along a pathway, the dogs may find the poor child before a human did. There were many villages, towns, and city-states that had been built at various points along the river. The chances that a baby would float all the way to the sea would be slim, someone would be bound to spot the mini ark and rescue it. Which in Sargon's case, someone did. In fact it could have been a periodic occurrence. The Euphrates is a long river, 1,740 miles long, so mothers (or fathers) wishing to give their child up for adoption may have resorted to the mini-ark method. After all, it worked very well for Noah in the first instance—God was with him and brought him safely to his new location and life—and so it's not hard to see how a Mesopotamian parent may reason.

The mother of Moses was in Egypt not Mesopotamia, true! But her family was from Mesopotamia and they would know the story of Noah well, and most likely the story of Sargon too, and any other babies that were set afloat. Romulus (who is given credit for founding Rome) and his twin brother Remus, were abandoned by their parents who placed them in a reed basket and set them afloat on the river Tiber. The story is a legend but allows us to see that in antiquity setting a baby afloat in a reed basket was a scenario people would identify with. The infant Moses was set afloat on the river Nile—his story cannot be discounted simply because baby Sargon was also set afloat on the river Euphrates.

Chapter 4

Educating Moses

And there went a man of the house of Levi, and took to wife a daughter of Levi.

—EXOD 2:1 KJV

THE SIMPLICITY WITH WHICH the book of Exodus announces the father and mother of Moses is worthy of note. We find a disarming candor that is unlike other literature, ancient or modern. Information is passed on to us void of any flowery embellishments and we get it like it is, or rather, like it was. The text may have a straightforward objective but its method is not without subtleties: neither of Moses's parents are named until we are well into the book of Exodus. The reason we are not told the parents' names at this point inclines us to the feeling that we are being told to "watch this." In the first few verses of chapter 2 there are quite a number of people mentioned but not one of them is named until we get to Moses. That is the first name we hear, and of course it has the literary effect of placing Moses in a spotlight: he is the one to keep our eyes on, watch this man because something is going to happen.

In the book *Genesis for Ordinary People* we learned that the year of the exodus was 1406 BC, we also know that Moses was 80 years old when he negotiated with Pharaoh for the release of the Israelites. So let's add the 80 years on to the date of the exodus and we arrive at the birth of Moses in 1486 BC. Reigning in Egypt at that point was Thutmose II, sometimes called Thutmosis II. Around the 18th and 19th Dynasties of Egyptian monarchs the words Mose or Mesu or Mases were a popular part of someone's name. They meant "born of" or "son of." Thutmose meant born of Thut, and Thut was the Egyptian god of moon, science, magic, speech, and writing. In the 19th Dynasty we meet Ramesses, meaning "son of Ra." Ra was the Egyptian sun god. The word *mose* seems to be derived from an Egyptian verb meaning "to produce" or "to draw forth." Exodus chapter 2 explains that Pharaoh's daughter named the baby she found in the river Nile "Moses," saying, "I drew him out of the water." In other words, the father of the baby in the river was unknown so he couldn't be the son of a named individual. He was drawn from the water not from a man or god, so he was simply named Mose, or Moses as the name has been passed down to us through Latin. The name also ties in well with the job that Moses was given because it was he who drew the Israelites out of Egypt.

Stephen in the New Testament informs us that "Moses was instructed in all the wisdom of the Egyptians" (Acts 7:22). The Egyptians held education in high esteem and had several schools, the most prestigious of which was the Prince's School, which undertook the education of Pharaoh's household, and Moses became a privileged son of that household.

There used to be a school of skeptical thought that taught that Moses could not have written the early books of the Bible because writing had not been invented at the time of Moses. During the years in which this theory was taught archaeology was in its infancy, but as archaeology matured it was quickly realized that the late invention of writing was simply untrue. Humans have been writing since before 3000 BC, and the writing first appears in Mesopotamia. The writing was cuneiform, which is based on syllables and ideograms. We learn in the book of Genesis that the LORD God was active in southern Mesopotamia, men called out his name; he spoke with men, and helped and advised them.

Moses entered the educational system at an important time in the history of the written word. What had formerly been writing based on syllables and signs was about to change to writing based on the alphabet. The importance of this change for the progress of human affairs cannot be overstated. It was a very important juncture in human history. And once again we find that the LORD God is there in the middle of the transition. God was active when writing began among men as a syllabic-based form of written communication and as the syllabic form was being reinvented to writing based on the alphabet he is there again. In fact, one of the first acts we see God do once the Israelites are out of Egypt is write. God is a writer! He wrote with his own hand on two tablets of stone. Jesus is also a writer; we only get a small glimpse of Jesus writing but write he did (John 8:6). So, we get two small windows to look through to see both Yahweh and Jesus writing.

"Did Moses write the Pentateuch?" This question has been asked for the last few centuries by those who theorize that the Pentateuch (the first five books of the Bible) is a composite work of four groups of people represented by the letters J., E., D., and P. "J" being the Yahwists (from the German Jahweh). "E" is for the Elohist. "D" is the source called the Deuteronomist, and "P" is the Priestly strand. This theory is known as the Documentary Hypothesis. So, I can at least agree with a part of their theory because, no, Moses did not write all of Exodus: God wrote some of it too.

Writing is beginning to look like a very important pursuit for humans to take seriously. God wants men to be able to write because reading is one important way he is going to communicate to people throughout the course of human history.

Chapter 5

The Problem With Large Numbers

THIS BOOK IS SUBTITLED *Unwrapping the Second Book of the Bible,* and we find that there is some unwrapping to do. A person interested in researching the book of Exodus does not have to look too far before he or she encounters objections to the exodus itself. The large number of people who are said to have marched out of Egypt en masse, has received a lot of critical cynicism. According to Exodus 12:37, there were about 600,000 men on foot, besides women and children. The first chapter in the book of Numbers explains that men who are over the age of 20 are considered ready for battle, and Exodus 13:18 tells us that the Israelites exited Egypt ready for battle. So we are probably talking about 600,000 men over the age of 20. Furthermore, many countries in the world with a high birth rate can have up to 50 percent of their population under the age of 20. And we know the Israelites were in that category, because what initially alarmed the Egyptians was the high birth rate of the Israelites (Exod 1:9). So if we include people under the age of 20 that would give us a figure near to 1.2 million taking part in the procession out of Egypt. We still need to add women and most likely elderly men. So we are talking about close to 2 million people, as critics of the book of Exodus seem happy to point out. Apparently, they also tell us that 2 million people marching say, 10 abreast, would have formed a line 150 miles long. That's startling. So I did some of my own calculations and I concluded that 2 million people walking 10 abreast forms a line that lasts for 113 miles, presuming each person was walking 3 feet from the person in front of them. Whatever the distance of the line, the logistics would be hard to implement and the number of marshals needed to keep the line moving and moving in an orderly manner must be high for so many people. Objections to this large number seem fairly obvious. The exodus of so many people in such a short space of time would be a logistical nightmare.

We also must consider that the Israelites left Egypt armed for battle, and over 600,000 Israelite men ready to fight would have been a formidable army by ancient (or modern) standards. Yet a little later in the exodus story the Egyptians chased the Israelites with 600 top-of-the-range chariots plus some other chariots of lesser quality. We don't know how many of the lesser quality chariots there were but when King Shishak of Egypt invaded Israel in around 940 BC he had 1,200 chariots. The exodus was held in 1406 BC when Amenhotep II was reigning, which was 466 years earlier, so Amenhotep II was unlikely to have too many other chariots. But let's say there was a generous total of 2,000 Egyptian chariots, and remembering that chariots are a useful piece of kit in warfare, even so, they are not going to make too much of a dent in an army of 600,000.

There are also the time constraints to consider: according to Galatians 3:17 there were 430 years from the promise first being given to Abram until the law was introduced. (The law and the exodus were roughly about the same time.) We can work out that 220 of those years were spent mostly in Canaan (as the Septuagint in Exodus 12:40 relates), and the other 210 years were in Egypt.

There were 70 persons accounted for who settled down in Egypt (Exod 1:5), though 75 according to the Septuagint, which Stephen quotes from in the New Testament. We know that two of the 75 people were female: Jacob's daughter Dinah and his granddaughter Serah, and most of the others were sons and grandsons. There would also be Jacob's sons' wives and most likely some of the grandsons also had wives by this time. So let us double the figure of 75 and make it 150 people (to account for females) for the first community of Israelite people who settled in Egypt. Now let's do an equation: 150 people with each couple producing 7 children, with a 40-year generation turnover, (remembering that it takes two people to produce offspring and that eventually the former generation will die), the population after 210 years would be about 22,500 people—a long way off 2 million people.

You, the reader, may be expecting me, the writer, to highlight a solution that makes good sense. And you would be correct in thinking that, because there is an explanation that makes good sense.

Chapter 6

The First Alphabet

THE BEGINNINGS OF THE alphabet are intriguing, and Jacob's family was right there in the thick of it. *Encyclopaedia Britannica* confirms that the Sinaitic inscriptions date from approximately the beginning of the 16th century BC.[1] Our current alphabet can be considered a continuation of the original alphabet created 3,500 years ago. Signs for syllables were being replaced by single letters, and the new form of writing was remarkably simple to implement—answers to puzzling questions may seem simple when you know the answer. The Egyptians had used hieroglyphics, which I'm sure most of us have seen at some point, and they also used a shorthand version called hieratic script. The Sumerians and Akkadians in Mesopotamia used cuneiform script, which, in its early stages, used a series of pictograms to record information. Cuneiform script is one of the earliest known systems of writing. It is recognized by its wedge-shaped marks on clay tablets, made by means of a blunt reed for a stylus. As cuneiform developed the written symbols began to equate to syllables. There were about 600 signs that were used on a regular basis to write using cuneiform script. Six hundred signs seems a little cumbersome compared to our current writing system which uses an alphabet of only 26 letters, and the early alphabet that had 22 letters.

The groundbreaking system used to identify the sounds attached to each letter of the early alphabet is where the simplicity comes in, because it is the same system we use to teach young children to read. You may have

1. *Encyclopaedia Britannica Online*, s.v. "Sinaitic Inscriptions," http://www.britannica.com/topic/Sinaitic-inscriptions.

seen a parent and child huddled over a book saying, "a is for apple, b is for ball, c is for cat" and so on. The system takes the initial letter of each word to make its point. The early alphabet was similar. The first letter was *aleph*, which means ox, and was symbolized by the simple picture of an ox's head. The illustration was easy to recognize because an ox has horns, and the letter was also quick and easy to write down. The sound it represented was the first part of the word aleph, which we know in English as the glottal stop sound: a kind of breathy "aah." The second letter of the early alphabet was *beth*, which means house. We have all heard of Bethlehem, which means "house of bread." A number of place names mentioned in the Bible begin with beth and they all mean house of something. Bethel means "house of God," beth for "house," and *el* for God. The alphabetic symbol for beth was a plan view of a house: a rectangle with a gap in it. The gap was where the door into the house would be. The sound that beth represented was "b," which is its initial letter. So instead of saying, "a is for apple and b is for ball," parents all those years ago would say, "aah is for aleph and b is for beth." The technical name for this writing system is acrophonic. Coping with 22 letters is simple and a lot less fussy than writing hundreds of syllables. Words and sentences could now be written down efficiently and speedily. A writer only needed to know what word he wanted to write and then assign the symbol to each letter in the word.

The first two letters of that first alphabet are where we get the word "alphabet," from aleph and beth. The spelling has changed slightly because it passed through a few cultures before it reached us in the twenty-first century—when the Greeks borrowed the letter aleph they called it *alpha*, and they called beth *beta*. Our capital letter A is also not too far away from the original ox's head pictograph, which somehow got turned upside down, but when we write A we are harkening back to those very early days of alphabetic writing.

A written language using the alphabet proved to be easier for those writing it than learning a host of symbols for syllables. However, the early writers used only consonants in their alphabet and no vowels. That may seem a little odd to us these days but it wasn't a big problem early on. Our modern minds would immediately point to words that share the same set of consonants but not the same vowels, words like "blind," "bland," and "blend." If these words were written down using only consonants they would look identical: "blnd." But this was not so much of a problem in the early days as we might imagine. The correct word was placed into the mind of the reader by the context of the sentence structure. For instance,

ppl expct blnd ppl t crry wht stcks

When the early books of the Bible were first written, words that shared the same consonants were identifiable because of their context. In early Hebrew the word "troop" or "clan" can be written using "lp." When Gideon spoke about his clan or troop being the smallest in Israel, "lp" were originally the two consonants that were used to write the word "clan." (The Hebrew word is *alpe*.) The precise number of people required for a clan or troop is not necessarily a fixed number. Troop is an indeterminate number of men; it could be 10 men, or quite a number more. The Egyptian platoon was 50 men. The platoon was made up of squads of 10 men.[2] If squad equates to the Hebrew troop we may be able to be more precise, but the word troop seems to leave room for maneuvering and the word clan certainly does. In the Amarna Letters (sometimes called the Amarna Tablets), written about 60 years or so after the exodus, we read that a troop could possibly be 10 men or more.[3]

But "lp" can have another meaning which has differing vowels, though when originally written only had the consonants; the other meaning of "lp" is "thousand." (The Hebrew word is *eleph*.) And to make matters slightly more complicated there is another meaning of "lp," which is "leader." Leader, again, uses different vowels but the same consonants. (The Hebrew word is *aluph*, derived from "aleph" meaning "ox" because a leader is as strong as an ox.)

When the book of Exodus was hot off the press its first readers would not have had a problem deciphering meanings because the context made it plain: the people reading the first few copies of Exodus would be aware of approximately how many people there were in Israel, they would know if "lp" referred to a small grouping such as a clan or a thousand. Historian Lina Eckenstein informs us that the early Hebrew word for thousand can also be translated as "families or tent-settlement."[4]

2. Partridge, *Fighting Pharaohs*, 88.

3. In the Amarna Tablets we read that the Byblos ruler Rib-Addi, a faithful vassal of Egypt, requests help from Egypt by asking them to send the household troops. But how many men are actually in a troop we are not able to determine. There is one occasion when Rib-Addi asks for 10 men. Sayce, "Letters by Rib-Addi," lines 17–19. So perhaps that is a troop, but there are other occasions when he asks for other numbers of men.

4. Eckenstein, *History of Sinai*, 73.

So we understand that if we translate "lp" as "clan" we are talking about a small grouping of people. But as time wore on and the actual events themselves described in the exodus became distant history, context would then be more of an issue. An example of context being slightly blurred is found in 1 Samuel 23:23 where the New International Version uses the phrase "among the clans of Judah" but the New American Standard Bible uses the phrase "among all the thousands of Judah." The word "leader" could be the meaning of "lp" too, but it is plain to see "leader" is out of context in this instance and cancels itself out. However, there seems to be some question in the minds of translators regarding the original word's meaning being either "clan" or "thousand."

Let us presume for a moment that when the book of Exodus was first written the phrase in chapter 12:37 which is usually translated as "600 thousand" actually meant "600 clans," or "600 troops" and presuming each clan had 10 men, the number would be 6,000 men. We suddenly have a manageable and realistic number of men leaving Egypt, and if we extrapolate the older men, and women and children, we end up with a number of about 20,000 to 22,000 people, not 2 million. The early readers of the book of Exodus were basically aware of how many compatriots they had and if the early numbers in the newly founded country of Israel were in the thousands rather than millions then reading "lp" as "clan" would be obvious to them.

Chapter 7

Dynasty

Moses was educated in all the wisdom of the Egyptians and was powerful in
speech and action.

—ACTS 7:22

MIRIAM, THE SISTER OF baby Moses, was bold enough to approach Pharaoh's
daughter and consequently played a part in securing a comprehensive, state
of the art, education for her brother, who would now be brought up in
the royal household and educated accordingly—to a very high academic
standard. The ancient Egyptians knew the importance of education and the
height of their academic system was the Prince's School, which undertook
the education of Pharaoh's household. In addition, some royal children had
personal tutors. Moses also had his biological mother and sister near him
during his tender years, and it appears they were keen to share their knowledge with him.

People sometimes ask which pharaoh was in power during the book
of Exodus's unfolding story. Egyptian history is fairly well documented,
though not perfect, but we have enough information to follow a timeline
through the book of Exodus, coupled with Egyptian history, enabling us to
work out who was in power at different intervals during the life of Moses.
First of all we need to set a datum line—a solid reference point—from which
to work. In my previous book, *Genesis for Ordinary People*, I calculated the

biblical timeline using the Septuagint, which is the Greek version of the Old Testament. When using the Septuagint to date events (e.g., the Flood) the biblical date tied in well with the date geological evidence gave us. We find a similar correlation between the book of Exodus and Egyptian history if we use the Septuagint.

The Septuagint was the version of the Old Testament the early church used and New Testament writers often quote it. The Septuagint is also the oldest manuscript of the Old Testament that we have, being centuries older than the Masoretic text, which is Hebrew but has some variations with the Septuagint, one of which is the numbers used.

Stephen, in Acts 7:14, chooses the number 75 for the number of people who went to Egypt, because he's read it in the Septuagint, even though the Masoretic text has the number 70. From this we can see that in New Testament times the Christians were reading the Septuagint and considered it accurate enough to quote. So once we follow the Septuagint numerically we find that the narrative of the book of Exodus follows pretty well with the Egyptian timeframe we get from historians.

First Kings 6:1 informs us that construction of the temple of the LORD began 440 years after the Israelites left Egypt. (The Masoretic text has 480 years but there may be a footnote in some versions of the Bible at 1 Kings 6:1 informing the reader that the Septuagint [which is abbreviated as LXX] has 440.)

So 1 Kings 6:1 is a good datum line to work from because the date 966 BC is fairly well attested as the year that work started on the temple, which informs us the exodus occurred in 1406 BC. We also know the age of Moses at various points of his life and that will help us. The Septuagint in Exodus 12:40 and the New Testament in Galatians 3:17 informs us that from the promise given to Abraham in the Mesopotamian city of Ur there were 430 years until the exodus occurred and the written law was issued. This means there were 430 years in which Abraham and his offspring would be strangers in Canaan and Egypt. Once we know that the exodus occurred in 1406 BC we can work out the year Abraham met Yahweh in the city of Ur, which was 1836 BC. Working out the timeframe of Isaac, Jacob, Joseph, and other family members at various points of their lives is also fairly easy.

When Jacob, at the age of 130, stood before Pharaoh the year would be 1616 BC. This is a period in Egyptian history when the Hyksos were ruling. The names of the Hyksos seem to be Semitic and there is general agreement that the Hyksos were from the Levant and surrounding areas.

One pharaoh from the Hyksos rule was called Jacob-Baal and another Ya-kobam.[1] To put it bluntly, the Hyksos were foreigners and this may have been irksome to native Egyptians, although, from Jacob's point of view we can see some providence working in his favor. The reign of the Hyksos in Egypt didn't last too long but while it did last it may well have made a pharaoh, who was one of the Hyksos, favorably disposed towards Jacob and his family as they, too, were of Semitic descent. The running order of pharaohs during the Hyksos period is one section of Egyptian history that is less well documented, perhaps owing to the fact that Egyptian pharaohs had a propensity for erasing information about predecessors they were unhappy with. However, the name of the pharaoh who admitted Joseph into government could be Pharaoh Khyan. He reigned at the height of the Hyksos's power. Egyptologists have different starting points for the beginning of his reign but most of them say he was in power in Egypt in the second half of the 1600s BC. Pharaoh Khyan is one of the better-attested kings from the Hyksos period, known from many seals and seal impressions. (Kings used personal seals as a means of authentication. Their seals made an impression in wax, clay, or other medium.) Historians assign varying lengths of time for Pharaoh Khyan's rule, usually from between 25 years, up to 50 years, as assigned by the 3rd century BC Egyptian historian Manetho. Looking at the evidence, the Bible student is left with the impression that Pharaoh Khyan's criteria for being the pharaoh in power when Joseph was admitted into government is strong—he was a pharaoh who was ruling in the later 1600s BC and one whose reign lasted 25 or more years. Pharaoh Khyan looks like the correct candidate.

The Hyksos were eventually overthrown and expelled from Egypt in the 1500s BC, and a new era—the 18th Dynasty—arose. The pharaohs of this new ruling class were native to Egypt, meaning that once again Egyptians were ruling Egypt. The expulsion of the Hyksos was a protracted affair but ultimately, with the rise of the 18th Dynasty, Egypt was finally free from being ruled by the Hyksos. However, the new 18th Dynasty monarchs were probably apprehensive about the possibility of the Hyksos regrouping and mounting a counterattack.

When Exodus says, "Now there arose up a new king over Egypt, which knew not Joseph" (Exod 1:8 kjv), the emphasis is on the word "new," because

---

1. Bigelow, "List of Pharaohs," sec. 13, lines 21–22. The Hyksos were in power during the 15th and 16th Egyptian Dynasties as well as a portion of the 17th Dynasty. The time the Hyksos were ruling in Egypt is known as the Second Intermediate Period.

it was in fact a new dynasty that had arisen after the Hyksos were finally expelled from the land. Pharaoh Ahmose was the founder of the 18th Dynasty. Ahmose's father had begun the tenacious and prolonged battle to expel the Hyksos, and lost his life as a result. Ahmose took up the challenge where his father left off and completed the conquest of the Hyksos. The Hyksos were still considered a threat and Pharaoh Ahmose may have been unhappy to see Jacob's descendants growing apace as the possibility of the burgeoning Israelite community aligning themselves with the Hyksos, in any future attempt by the Hyksos to regain power was a particular worry for him. This scenario was not beyond the bounds of possibility—Exodus 1:9–10 puts it like this: "'Look,' he said to his people, 'the Israelites have become far too numerous for us. Come, we must deal shrewdly with them or they will become even more numerous and, if war breaks out, will join our enemies, fight against us and leave the country.'" The Hyksos and Israelites both being of Semitic descent was a major concern for Pharaoh Ahmose. This is where enslavement began for the descendants of Jacob, the date would be around 1550 BC.

The parcel of Egyptian land that had originally been provided for Jacob and his family by the Hyksos pharaoh was called the land of Goshen, in Greek it was called Gesem. The Israelites first acquired the land by a helpful tip from Joseph to his father. Joseph said,

> When Pharaoh calls you in and asks, "What is your occupation?" you should answer, "Your servants have tended livestock from our boyhood on, just as our fathers did." Then you will be allowed to settle in the region of Goshen, for all shepherds are detestable to the Egyptians. (Gen 46:33–34)

Joseph's advice to his father was not only a caution about the Egyptian people's attitude toward strangers (which may have already been showing signs of strain with the Hyksos in power), but the advice was also a piece of diplomacy enabling them to claim independent status. They let Pharaoh know they had their own livestock to support them, thereby informing the Egyptian people that Jacob's family members were not an ambitious group who wished to rise above their occupation as shepherds. The Egyptian grain farmers and agriculturalist workforce around the fertile Nile area worked hard on cultivating crops and making their land productive so they would not want shepherds with their wandering herds trampling upon their hard-worked land. Egyptians were not keen on pastoralists and as a consequence Jacob's family was given land in what is the western end of the Wadi Tumilat, on the eastern side of the Nile delta, a little further north from where the Wadi Tumilat ends. The Wadi Tumilat lies towards the end of the "way to Shur," which the book of Genesis tells us was a route taken by people when they travelled to Egypt from Canaan. The Israelites were located not too far from the route that would get them back home—they were not intending to stay in Egypt.

The expulsion of the Hyksos saw some political upheaval in Egypt, and policies made were not favorable to the descendants of Jacob's family members. Josephus says the children of Israel were taken away from their normal work and forced to do a number of jobs, which included digging canals from the Nile, building flood barriers, helping with various building projects, and learning mechanical skills of many sorts. The book of Exodus mentions the Israelites building Pithom and Rameses as store cities for Pharaoh. The word Rameses can be applied to an area or a person, at this stage in Egyptian chronology the famous pharaoh, "Ramesses the Great" had not yet been born, he came along 200 years later. The Septuagint mentions one more city that the Hebrews worked on—The city of On or Heliopolis, as it was called in Greek. The city of On was located about 30 miles to the south from where the Israelites were located, slightly northeast of modern-day Cairo.

The Wadi Tumilat has been the subject of archaeological studies since the early 1900s AD and two sites (or "tells," as they are known among archaeologists) have been put forward as the probable cities mentioned in Exodus. Which city is which has been a point of debate, though Tell el-Retaba seems to be favored as Pithom. The latest researchers say there is still a lot to be discovered there. In 2012 the remains of an early 18th Dynasty settlement were found.[2] Recently unearthed architectural remains of buildings and storage structures from the early 18th Dynasty have also been found.[3] This is the correct timeframe for the forced labor of the Israelites. Pharaoh Ahmose put the Israelites to work and this state of affairs lasted for about 40 years until events took a turn for the worse.

Pharaoh Thutmose was the third pharaoh of the 18th Dynasty and ruled until about 1482 BC.[4] Thutmose tried to secure his reach all the way north to Syria, probably because the rule of the Hyksos had been a worrying

2. Hudec et al, "Tell el-Retaba," lines 7–8.

3. Hudec and Dubcova, "Discoveries," lines 1–2, 6–10.

4. *Encyclopaedia Britannica Online*, s.v. "Thutmose I: King of Egypt." http://www. britannica.com/EBchecked/topic/594485/Thutmose-I.

period for indigenous Egyptians and they wanted to make sure the Hyksos, or any other people group, wouldn't take over their land again.

The enslavement of the Israelites had not worked in slowing down their population boom, as the last few decades had shown to Pharaoh Thutmose. Removing the Israelite men from the Israelite women for periods of time, so the men could work on various Egyptian projects, should have had the byproduct of slowing down the growth of the Israelite population, but it did not. Exodus 1:22 says, "Then Pharaoh gave this order to all his people: 'Every Hebrew boy that is born you must throw into the Nile, but let every girl live.'" Thutmose's wife was Queen Ahmose, who held the title of "Great Royal Wife," and their offspring included a girl named Hatshepsut, who was no ordinary child. Hatshepsut eventually became pharaoh herself, but not until 1479 BC.[5] Thutmose and his official wife had four children: two boys and two girls. The two boys and one girl died, leaving Princess Hatshepsut as the only child of the royal couple.

Moses was born in 1486 BC, during the reign of Pharaoh Thutmose, so at that time Hatshepsut would have been known as Pharaoh's daughter. Thutmose died in 1482 BC, not long after the birth of Moses. Hatshepsut was a thoroughbred daughter of King Thutmose and his royal wife Queen Ahmose, but the royal pair had not left a living son. This is where the royal harem came in handy because there was a male son who was royal issue from Thutmose's actual body and a respected secondary queen. But the young Prince Thutmose II needed to shore up his royal credentials so it was thought prudent for him to marry his half-sister Hatshepsut. Thutmose II took the throne in 1482 BC. His reign did not last long—there are some differences of opinion on just how long, but the facts, as far as the book of Exodus is concerned, tie in well if we go with the short-reign option of a mere three years of rule.[6] Some of the pharaohs' offspring did not enjoy good health and interbreeding closely did not help matters.

5. Wilson, "Queen," para. 2.
6. Tyldesley, "Hatshepsut," lines 39–41.

Chapter 8

All Manner of Rigorous Service

WHEN WE READ ABOUT Moses and his family in the book of Exodus the story has become so ingrained within us that we see it as a major event in Egyptian history, but the reality is, yes, Moses's story had massive far reaching effects, but at the time it took place Moses was not a large part of what was going on in Egypt. He was tucked away as an adopted son of Hatshepsut, people probably didn't take much notice of him, because there could be quite a number of children attached to the royal household in one way or another and Moses was simply one more. We see a similar picture when God placed Joseph close to the center of the Hyksos Egyptian pharaoh and his government. Joseph wiled away his early years in prison, off the radar until he was needed. But in the 1400s BC the Hyksos were no longer in power, and yet God had a way of planting a young Hebrew close to the center of the new 18th Dynasty. Moses spent his early years hidden in the depths of the royal household until a higher authority needed him.

Moses must have felt some affection for his adopted mother Hatshepsut, and the lady herself is thought to have been an exceptional woman. She claimed the top position in what had previously been an occupation predominated mostly by men. Hatshepsut was one of the few female pharaohs of Egypt, and what a fine job she made of it too. During her reign Egypt enjoyed years of peace and prosperity. She initiated building projects that surpassed those undertaken by previous pharaohs. Her reign was essentially free of warfare, perhaps because her foreign policy was largely based on trade. She ruled for about 22 years before her death occurred in

1457 BC. Her mummy has recently been found and an abscess of the gum is thought to have killed her. These days, a course of antibiotics would have helped to heal the infection.

Thutmose III took over the throne of Egypt after the death of Hatshepsut. He was the son of Thutmose II and a secondary harem wife, whose name was Isis. In the league table of the king's harem wives, Isis languished in the bottom half of the table. She was not very high up, which is a further reason that Hatshepsut became pharaoh, because technically Hatshepsut was co-regent with Thutmose III, who was only a boy and needed Hatshepsut's help in reigning. Before too long however, Hatshepsut declared herself pharaoh, which was allowed by the Egyptian elite, probably because she was doing a fine job and secondly because Thutmose III had a mother from the lower regions of the harem and a father who also had a mother from the harem. Conversely, Hatshepsut had bona fide royal descent from both, her father Thutmose, and her mother the "Great Royal Wife" Queen Ahmose. One Egyptologist says that Thutmose III developed a loathing for Hatshepsut[1] and at some point after Hatshepsut's death a valiant attempt was made to erase her name from Egyptian history. The blotting out of Hatshepsut's memory did not succeed, shown by the fact that we are speaking about her now. Thutmose III also wanted to secure the throne for his own offspring, so may have had no scruples about erasing the memory of Hatshepsut from Egyptian history.

The painstaking work of historians has helped us retrieve information about Hatshepsut. Reconstructing stonework and inscriptions has been an important part of being able to see back into Hatshepsut's life and times. There is a possibility that early historians may have been unaware of Hatshepsut's reign as pharaoh. Josephus, for instance, calls the princess who drew Moses out of the water Thurmuthis, which is close to her father's name, "Thutmose," and may have been a female variant. But Hatshepsut's name was omitted from the Kings List of Ramesses II, so even some of the later pharaohs may have been unaware of her existence.

Hatshepsut had given Moses his name and arranged for him to be brought up and schooled. Now that she was dead, Moses would be grieving to some extent, owing to the kindness shown to him and the kinship he felt to Hatshepsut.

Thutmose III, who was now in complete control, had received an excellent education, which included the military acumen of the preceding

1. Wilson, "Queen," 32–33.

pharaohs who knew a thing or two about warfare, having successfully rid the land of the Hyksos. Moses too, would have been taught this strategic knowledge of combat. We know that Thutmose III took part in military campaigns in Nubia, which is south of Egypt in Africa. Nubia was also called Ethiopia by the Greeks. We find that Josephus records Moses taking part in military campaigns in Ethiopia too. Moses may well have had a high position in the Egyptian army owing to his relationship to Hatshepsut. Josephus adds some more intriguing information by letting us know that on one of these Ethiopian outings Moses acquired an Ethiopian wife. Moses would be under the age of 40 so he's the right age to get married, and furthermore we read in Numbers 12:1 that Moses did in fact have an Ethiopian wife. There seems to have been a longstanding tradition connecting Ethiopia and the Jewish people. Where the relationship originated is open to question. More recently, in the 1900s AD, there were several waves of Ethiopian Jews taking up residence in the land of Israel. Perhaps the relationship between the two countries may have had its fledgling beginnings with Moses.

Acts chapter 7 tells us that Moses was 40 years old when the thought entered his head to pay a visit to his own people: the children of Israel. That would make it the year 1446 BC, and by that year his adopted mother was dead. Once Thutmose III was entirely on the throne, Moses may have felt little affinity to him, so his mind began to look elsewhere for familial contact. Something stirred inside the heart of Moses as he found himself motivated to see how Jacob's family members were doing. He probably remembered all he was told as a young boy by his true sister and his mother. Moses would be in the employ of Thutmose III at this time, and as employers go Thutmose III is reputed to be fair, level headed, and an excellent military strategist. He never lost a battle and would confound the enemy by taking the hard narrow road over a tough mountain pass while his opponents would be expecting him to send his troops along the main highways. Thutmose III followed his own mind when he thought he was right even when instructed to take a certain course of action by his generals or when he disagreed with his military strategists. All the men in his army shouted, "We follow thy Majesty whithersoever thy Majesty goes."[2] Thutmose III would lead his men along the hard path, climbing through a narrow pass to take his enemy unawares, and wait at the head of a pass until the last man was safely through.

2. Millmore, "Thutmose III," para. 8.

Egyptian military operations that Moses was involved in would teach him a great deal about strategy and warfare, lessons that would be useful to him later. But military campaigns took place only periodically, the rest of the time, the government, and many of the people who had been conscripted into the army, would have other work. When the area was at peace, mining operations would be scheduled. These were also undertaken periodically because copper, turquoise, and gold were valued materials for a kingdom to possess. The mines were further afield from the Nile delta in Nubia or Sinai. The land of Goshen, where the Israelites lived, was agreeably poised for travel to three main areas. The Wadi Tumilat made a natural path, and if the path were followed to the east for 40 or 50 miles, Lake Timsah would soon come into view. A crossroads would then appear and a choice of north, south, or straight on could be taken. The southern road led to the western side of the Sinai Peninsula where a copper and turquoise mine lay about 150 miles away at a mountain called Serabit el-Khadim. The southern route also offered another pathway: after following the southern path for 45 miles, a left turn along another pathway heading east could be taken, and this eastern pathway made its way 190 miles to another copper mine named Timna. Turning south at Timna would quickly bring a traveller into Midianite territory.

The Israelites, says the book of Exodus, were burdened with "all manner of service." The mechanical skills that Josephus mentioned could be partly linked to Egyptian mining operations. The Israelites certainly lived en route to a turquoise and copper mine, so it would be easier for the Egyptians to conscript a number of them for the mining expeditions. Mining can be a messy and dangerous business, and at this stage the Egyptians would have no qualms about sending a few Israelites into the mines. The King James Bible relates that the Egyptians enforced the Israelites to complete "all manner of service in the field: all their service, wherein they made them serve, *was* with rigour" (Exod 1:14). The Hebrew word for "field" can also be translated as "land" or "countryside" and the mines were "out there" in the countryside, although what the Egyptians meant by "countryside" and the picture a modern person living in the West has of "countryside" may be different. The mining expeditions would certainly be classed as "rigorous." Copper contained within rock would be dug out, then the rock, or ore as it is known, would be smelted. The smelting process is a skilled procedure and once copper has been extracted from the ore the copper can then be cast, which is also skilled work. Later in the book of Exodus we find that there were two particular Israelites, by the names of Bezalel and Oholiab, who were particularly skilled in various sorts of metal work. Aaron too had some knowledge of how to cast. Examples of early copper work reveal the metal was usually cast. The Egyptians mastered the art and learned that copper can be alloyed with a small amount of tin resulting in bronze which made the technique of casting easier to perform.

The mountain where the Sinai mine is located, Serabit el-Khadim, is not only famous for its ancient mines but it is also the place of the oldest known alphabetic writing, called Proto-Sinaitic script. The inscriptions are Semitic and closely linked to Proto-Canaanite script, which was a forerunner of Hebrew writing.

Chapter 9

Moses on the Run

THE STIRRINGS OF SAVING the Israelites and leading them to safety were already beginning to move in the heart of Moses. He felt enthused enough to go and visit his flesh and blood kin, where he would see exactly how the Israelites were recruited for their various work projects, and how they were supervised while they were working. There's every chance that Moses made the visit while he was on official business, he may even have requested some sort of position as an overseer for the work of the Israelites.

When Joseph first arrived in Egypt and the Hyksos were in power they ruled from Avaris, a city that is close to the land of Goshen. Pharaoh Ahmose, the founder of the 18th Dynasty, fought off the Hyksos and when he finally removed them from Egypt he destroyed the Hyksos citadel at Avaris. Pharaoh Ahmose ruled from Upper Egypt in Thebes, which was about 480 miles south of Avaris following the river Nile. However, according to the recent archaeological work being done at Avaris[1] (now called Tell el-Daba, just south of modern-day Qantir), during the 18th Dynasty enormous storage facilities were set up and among them were numerous silos, including at least 30 round grain silos.[2] This will probably ring a bell with people who've read Exodus chapter 1 because the Israelites worked on Rameses as a storage city. People sometimes make the mistake of connecting the famous Pharaoh, Ramesses the Great, with the city of Rameses,

1. Austrian, Tell el-Daba, lines 6–11.
2. Bietak, "Palatial Precinct," para. 12.

thinking he was the pharaoh involved in the exodus story, but he reigned in 1279 BC, much too late to be involved in the exodus or the city of Avaris where the Israelites built the storage facilities. Pharaoh Ahmose had a son called Ramose, which informs us that the Egyptians were using the name Ramose (born of Ra, the sun god) during the early 18th Dynasty. Avaris was the name of the city while the Hyksos ruled. It's likely that Pharaoh Ahmose would want to remove all traces of the Hyksos. (The ancient Egyptians did have a tendency towards removing all traces of something they weren't happy about.) So Pharaoh Ahmose could have named the storage city he ordered to be built after his son Ramose. Prince Ramose seems to disappear, so if he died the newly rebuilt city would be a memorial to him. Either way Rameses is what the Bible says the area was called, both in Genesis and Exodus.

People sometimes look for reasons to distrust the Bible, but if we believe the Bible, there is a route through general history and archaeology that makes sense and ties in well with the Bible's narrative. We have to follow the thread, just like the Israelites made their way slowly through the wilderness from place to place and finally got safely out into Canaan. If we too follow the thread we can see how events happened both biblically and also from a historical and an archaeological perspective. We believe the Bible because God has breathed on it, not because every small point can be proved. Faith must come first, but once faith is in place we begin to find that historical accuracy is also there when we look from the correct angle.

When Pharaoh Ramesses the Great (Ramesses II) came along 200 years later, Avaris (the city of Rameses), where the storage facilities were, eventually became absorbed into the new city of Pi-Ramesses, which Pharaoh Ramesses the Great enlarged and rebuilt. But we know that Rameses was a district in the region of Goshen (Gen 47:11, 27). Genesis refers to Joseph and Jacob settling in the district of Rameses because when Genesis and Exodus were written the readers would understand where Rameses was, even though the city was called Avaris when Joseph and Jacob first moved there.

Furthermore, the area of Avaris has in recent years been subject to extensive archaeological work and we know that Pharaoh Ahmose began the work on the storage facilities soon after the expulsion of the Hyksos. The storage silos were used to store enormous quantities of grain for a considerable number of people. All the facts seem to point to a military facility, especially as the Hyksos had been pushed out to the east, troops would need to garrison the eastern delta in case there were reprisals from the Hyksos or any other invaders. These Egyptian troops would need a steady supply of food, so the silos were built to provide the Egyptian forces with their necessary provisions. As time went on and the Hyksos did not reappear, the area of Rameses was then used to build palaces for the Thutmose clan. The two palaces that have been found have a fine symmetrical design. The larger palace is about 200 meters by 100 meters. These weren't built until Thutmose III's reign, so Moses may have been stationed there for the purpose of overseeing the building project in some way. He would be able to visit his relatives quite easily. Some of the Israelites may have been involved in the construction of the palaces.

Let us go back to the time Moses was born for a moment. The Thutmose family was obviously thinking of a palace based in Avaris/Rameses and so Thutmose I, who, it seems, issued the order to destroy the Hebrew boys would be either on a visit there or already had a base there, but most likely on a visit. His attention would be drawn to the Hebrews and the problem of their population growth, because of his proximity to them; hence, the dastardly order was quickly issued.

Moses was born around that time. Princess Hatshepsut would be with the royal touring party and probably bathed in the Nile because her attendants had no place to prepare her normal bathing routine as they did in the palace at Thebes. Providentially, the infant Moses was floating in the river at that precise time. After Hatshepsut's slave girl retrieved the baby, Miriam approached Hatshepsut and as a result Miriam was able to procure work for her mother as the baby's nurse. Some English versions of the Bible appear to say that the mother of the baby took the child away from the princess and brought the baby back some time later. But if the section is read in Hebrew, the princess says, take this child, similar to a mother having a baby in her arms and asking you to "Take my baby while I do my shopping," and you are left holding the baby. Getting the picture of what actually happened: it looks like Jochabed, the mother of Moses (Exod 6:20) was offered the job of nursing the child, and suddenly found herself as one of Hatshepsut's attendants. She took the baby from Hatshepsut, and nursed him while Hatshepsut paid her wages as a member of the staff. Jochabed may have found herself on the way to Thebes as a part of the deal because the main royal residence was based there (or possibly Memphis, which acted as a second capital in Lower Egypt). Hatshepsut wouldn't want to let the baby go far from her view, her heartstrings had already been touched by the vulnerability of the young child, so letting baby Moses go away to some undisclosed area of Goshen seems unlikely. Thebes was closer to Nubia too, where Moses found a wife when he was older.

Back in Avaris/Rameses where Thutmose III is building his palaces, Moses was not impressed by the methods the Egyptian foremen used to make sure the Israelite workforce buckled down to some work. He saw one particular Egyptian beating a Hebrew, so Moses made sure there were no other Egyptians close by and, using his acquired knowledge of armed conflict, quickly dispatched the Egyptian from the land of the living and buried him in the sand. This was a calculated act of resistance by Moses, as he took time to look around, keeping his wits about him. He appears to be setting himself up as a militant leader for the oppressed people. He moved the Egyptian's body to where there was sand, the eastern Nile delta is fertile but the sand encroaches close by. When Moses wrote about his early years he recalled this episode and mentioned the specific type of burial place. Someone else writing may have written that the dead Egyptian was buried "in the ground," but Moses was precise and mentioned "the sand" because the incident was burned into his memory.

The next day Moses quickly realized that the community he was try-ing to reach out to did not recognize his leadership skills. The news of him killing the Egyptian was making the rounds, and soon the law enforcers of Pharaoh would hear of it. Sure enough, they did, the administration of the Egyptian judicial system was soon at work on this particular criminal case. Moses may have hung around for a short while, perhaps to prepare his Ethiopian wife for what may follow. Soon, Pharaoh's mandate was issued and Moses was sentenced to receive the death penalty for his crime. Thut-mose III may not have felt a great liking for Hatshepsut, but if the reports of him being a fair man are true, then Moses was being treated according to the law of Egypt and his sentence was not influenced by any animosity that Thutmose III felt for Moses's link to Hatshepsut.

Moses must have been aware of the dire circumstances he may find himself in and made provision for a hasty escape. He made his way to Lake Timsah, and once at the crossroads there he turned south for 45 miles and then took the eastern pathway to Timna, where the other copper mine was located. Once at the Timna mine, Midianite land would then be close if Moses turned south, he would then be on the eastern side of the Gulf of Aqaba. The Egyptian's were not yet using the Timna mine on any great scale so Moses would be out of reach.

The Midianites were descendants of Abraham and Keturah, so they would be acquainted with the stories of Abraham's journey with the Lord, and one of the first people Moses meets in Midian is a priest named Reuel. Moses had helped Reuel's daughters by looking after the girls' interests when some local shepherds with little regard for the girls or their flock were treating them shoddily. Moses was from Adam's stock and would still have some residue of strength that had been apportioned to the Adamic clan, along with his long years. God had said the years of those in Adam's line would be cut to 120 and so it was with Moses. Moses would live to be 120, considerably longer than many of the pharaohs but nowhere as long as the antediluvian members of Adam's family. But the remaining portion of strength, which though diminishing along with the long years of life, still helped him in making quick work of the Egyptian whom he killed. And now his strength also helped in putting a stop to the chauvinism of the shepherds who were stopping the Midianite young women water their flocks. We don't read that any of the shepherds were killed. Moses was learning fast, he didn't want that sort of trouble following him any further, but he was able to make a stand for the girls. Their father Reuel was surprised the girls were home so soon and so we see that the shepherds had been in the habit of making their work harder for some time.

Chapter 10

Food Distribution Network

REUEL AND MOSES BOTH shared Abraham as a common ancestor. Reuel's name has "el" for its last syllable, which indicates Reuel was familiar with the God of the Hebrews. He was also a priest and a respected man among the Midianites. Reuel gave his daughter Zipporah to Moses in marriage. She was probably young, indicated by the fact that Reuel's exasperation revealed itself when his daughters failed to offer Moses the common courtesy of the times after he had put himself at risk for the girls. Reuel probably said, "What are you girls playing at? Get back there and invite the man to have something to eat with us."

During Moses's Midianite residence we can't be sure what happened to his Ethiopian wife. Perhaps she made the journey to Midian with him—a man having more than one wife was not without precedent in Abraham's family. Moses related well to Reuel and quickly became a part of his family and settled down. Thoughts of rescuing his fellow Israelites from their oppressors in Egypt must have slowly subsided during the long years Moses was with Reuel's family.

Reuel appears to retire or die and his son Jethro takes over the family business. Some decades later we find that Jethro is now the man in charge. English Bibles refer to Jethro as Moses's father-in-law, but the Hebrew word used for father-in-law can be used of brother-in-law as well. The word has a wider application here, so Jethro was probably of a similar age to Moses and the two men were close confidants, relatives, and friends.

Decades passed, Moses must have felt quite settled in Midian. Moses played his part in the family business as a herdsman. Sheep and goats were the likely candidates for the flocks that Jethro's family traded in. We know from archaeological expeditions that the supervisors of the mine at Timna made sure their workers were well fed. "Somebody took care that these people were eating well," said Erez Ben-Yosef, an archaeologist from Tel Aviv University.[1] Sheep and goats were on the menu, their bones have been found with butchering marks on them. Other food was also prepared, some of which had to be imported from the Mediterranean Sea. A network of food distributors crisscrossed the landscape. There would have to be an infrastructure of which Jethro's family business was probably a part.

Moses had a reason for leading one of Jethro's flocks from Midian to the far side of the Sinai Peninsula. The link between the two areas is mining: the mine in Timna, situated very close to where Jethro's family lived, and the mine at Serabit el-Khadim on the far side of the wilderness from where Midian was located. The route between the two areas stretches some distance, and is not the easiest to traverse. The terrain of the Sinai Peninsula is not the place a shepherd would naturally take his flock for grazing. There was a reason Moses took his flock on a 116-mile journey and the reason may well have been that the animals accompanying him were part of a trade agreement. The mineworkers at Serabit el-Khadim also needed food and Moses was a small part of the distribution process.

Near the mountain called Serabit el-Khadim are two other mountains in close proximity to each other, with a sandy area nestled between them. The outstanding feature of Serabit el-Khadim is its twin peaks, which stand a little over 750 meters (nearly 2,500 feet) above sea level. There is a temple built on a part of the mountain dedicated to the Egyptian goddess Hathor, who was, among other things, the patron goddess of miners. Hathor is depicted as a cow or a humanoid female with bovine attributes. The temple is a tourist attraction in the modern world; it was hewn out of rock and is an impressive place to visit. Two other mountains, Jabal Sāniyah and Jabal Ghorâbi, reside near Serabit el-Khadim. Jabal or Gebel means mountain and it's used in some Arabic place names. The three mountains are within a few kilometers of each other. (They can been seen quite easily on Internet maps, getamap.net is a good place to view them.) Linguistically Jabal Sāniyah is similar to Mount Sinai, and Jabal Ghorâbi has a name that is

1. Gannon, "Workers," para 4.

close to Mount Horeb. Exodus 3:1 tells us that Moses came to a mountain called Horeb. If Jabal Ghorâbi is Horeb then it is located close to the sandy area that travellers would naturally walk through.

Back in Egypt, Pharaoh Thutmose III died around about 1425 BC, and Moses would be about 60 years of age at that point. Moses was outliving his Egyptian contemporaries and was still physically active. Pharaoh Thutmose's eldest son had died earlier so another son of his, called Amenhotep, took the throne. His name as pharaoh was Amenhotep II. This particular pharaoh not being a firstborn son is worthy of note because later in the story the firstborn Egyptian sons die but Pharaoh himself did not die as he was not a firstborn son.

Towards the end of chapter 2 in the book of Exodus the narrative speaks of the time Moses spent in Midian.

> During that long period, the king of Egypt died. The Israelites groaned in their slavery and cried out, and their cry for help because of their slavery went up to God. (Exod 2:23–24)

The Israelites had now been oppressed for some 125 years and the outlook was bleak: the new pharaoh, Amenhotep II, was not the type of man who would make life easier for them. We have access to the contents of a personal letter from Amenhotep II written by himself to his viceroy of Nubia, whose name was Usersatet. In the letter we see that Amenhotep II had a certain contempt for foreigners. The letter reads: "These people from Tekshi (Syria) are worthless—what are they good for?"[2] As well as his xenophobic advice, Amenhotep II also berates the viceroy for promoting a Nubian servant to a higher position: "Do not trust the Nubians, but beware of their people and their witchcraft. Take this servant of a commoner, for example, whom you made an official although he is not an official whom you should have suggested to His Majesty; or did you want to allude to the proverb: 'If you lack a gold battle-axe inlaid with bronze, a heavy club of acacia wood will do'? So, do not listen to their words and do not heed their messages!"[3]

Amenhotep II's physical prowess has also been written about. Inscriptions claim he could shoot an arrow through a copper target one palm thick, and that he was able to row his ship faster and farther than two hundred members of the navy could row theirs.[4] I guess it's left to our own mind to

2. Hornung, "Pharaoh," 291.
3. Ibid.
4. Gardiner, *Egypt*, 198.

decide whether these inscriptions are actually true. The king's athleticism also played a part in foreign affairs when he is said to have singlehandedly killed 7 rebel princes at Kadesh, which successfully terminated his first Syrian campaign on a victorious note. After the campaign, the king ordered the bodies of the 7 princes to be hung upside down on the prow of his ship.[5] These writings give us a small glimpse into the personality of Amenhotep II.

The 18th Dynasty began a fresh era in Egypt that Egyptologists call the New Kingdom. With Amenhotep II the dynasty would be on its 7th pharaoh. Amenhotep II was born and raised in Memphis,[6] located in Lower Egypt (lower because of the landscape: the river Nile starts at a higher elevation in the south, known as Upper Egypt, and gradually works its way to a lower elevation in the north). The traditional capital of Egypt had been in Thebes, located in Upper Egypt, but since the Hyksos ruled from Lower Egypt, the 18th Dynasty decided to fortify the Nile delta area and have a royal presence there. The Israelites were located to the east of the delta in Lower Egypt. Amenhotep II knew the area well and part of his duties as a prince was to oversee the deliveries of wood at the dockyard in Memphis. He was also designated High Priest over Lower Egypt.[7] Amenhotep II came to the throne early in life: he was 18 years of age when he took total control.

5. Grimal, *Ancient Egypt*, 218.
6. Gardiner, *Egypt*, 198.
7. Ibid.

Chapter 11

Mines Reveal Things Previously Hidden

THE ISRAELITES HAD BEEN crying out under their heavy load. This is a theme we may see in our own lives, people sometimes pray when life becomes a burden or when trouble hits them, and it seems that God in his wisdom may allow suffering into our lives because distress has a way of turning our attention to where it ought to be. There are a couple of words written in Romans 5:3 that tell us "suffering produces," and the Israelites, who were groaning under the weight placed on them by the Egyptian government, may not have realized that God was at work producing something that would be of value to the world.

> God looked on the Israelites and was concerned about them. (Exod 2:25)

Around the year 1410 BC, Jethro would have given Moses the task of taking some animals to the area around Serabit el-Khadim. The journey from Timna to Serabit el-Khadim was not the easiest to negotiate. From what is now called Timna Park, Moses would travel south for 6 miles and then follow a road west for about 60 miles to the city of Nekhel, the ancient capital of the Sinai province. From Nekhel, Moses, his flock, and probably a few other workers from Jethro's family who were helping Moses, would turn south southwest for about 50 miles, which would take them to the mountains of the Serabit el-Khadim area. When Moses reached his journey's end it appears the Egyptian contingent working on this particular mining expedition had not yet arrived. The mines were not in constant use, each mining excursion would be planned well in advance and when quotas of turquoise or copper were met, the expedition would be complete.

Moses stationed himself and his team in the general area and tried to keep his animals fed and watered while waiting for the arrival of the mining officials. It was at this point he saw a bush aflame. There are online photographs available of the Serabit el-Khadim area and among the points of interest are trees and scattered bushes on the landscape. It was one of these bushes that Moses noticed, located on Jabal Ghorâbi (Mount Horeb), which is a smaller mountain than Serabit el-Khadim but close by. Intrigued why the bush managed to stay ablaze for so long, Moses walked probably one or two kilometers (more or less a mile) to see what was attracting his attention. He appears to be by himself at this point, his other workers were probably looking after the sheep and goats, or resting. Exodus 3:3 in the King James Bible puts the incident like this: "And Moses said, I will now turn aside, and see this great sight, why the bush is not burnt."

We notice the bush was not on the general path but Moses needed to "turn aside," something we all need to do if we desire to see and hear the Lord. We also realize that Moses was an intelligent, inquisitive, and bold man. Some people, upon seeing a bush that did not burn up may have run in the opposite direction. But not Moses, he made his way to the bush where he is rewarded by hearing a voice,

"Moses Moses!" The voice was earnest, speaking his name twice.

Moses said, "Here I am" (Exod 3:4). The burning bush encounter yields much information not only for Moses but for us all.

"Don't come any closer" (Exod 3:5), said the voice.

Fire can burn, so Moses was advised to stay where he was. But this was no ordinary fire! True, but it was a blaze of some sort, though not from this world. (The bush itself was used as a vehicle, evangel, or angel through which God spoke [Exod 3:2].) A fire can warm us if we stay the correct distance from it, or burn us if we get too close. Some men can't cope with burning love, they know only selfishness, love is foreign to them and is too painful for them to put into practice—the fire that keeps a house warm can also burn the house to the ground.

The voice delivered its next bit of advice:

> Take off your sandals for the place you are standing is holy ground.
> (Exod 3:5)

Moses knew that in ancient times, removing footwear on entering a place to which respect was due, such as a temple, a palace, or even the private house of a great man, was a mark of respect and showed a willing humility to engage with the host. Moses is now entering into a celestial precinct that normally does not reveal itself in the natural world, he will understand that he is entering into the courts and presence of someone worthy of respect. But who?

> I am the God of your father, the God of Abraham, the God of Isaac and the God of Jacob. (Exod 3:6)

Thus, a new era begins.

Formerly, Yahweh had walked and talked with the patriarchs, he was accessible. Adam was chosen and brought up by him. Cain and Abel brought him gifts, Enoch walked with him, and Noah built an ark from plans given to him by Yahweh. When Noah and his family entered the boat, Yahweh was outside closing the door and probably applying the last small section of bitumen to seal the door. Abraham met Yahweh in the city of Ur, and met him again in Canaan, he had lunch with him and had an after-lunch walk where some serious discussion took place. Yahweh walked and talked on earth. In Genesis chapter 1 he spoke to the humans he had created and told them to move throughout the earth. It is little wonder that every culture seems to have a history of the divine being. As generations progressed some of the stories slowly changed, but still we see a shadow of truth in most of them.

God loved and worked with early man helping them move forward from hunter-gatherers into settled communities. Southern Mesopotamia is where Yahweh did some extensive work, planting the garden of Eden. Men in the south of Mesopotamia knew of him, similar to how we might know someone in our community who we catch a glimpse of every now and again and may even say "hello" to once in a while. The Akkadians (from southern Mesopotamia) called him Ea. The word is pronounced as E-ah or Ayah.[1] If the E sound is soft we hear the Hebrew sounding Yah—a shortened version of Yahweh, as in hallelu"jah." Yahweh instructed Moses to tell the Israelites that "I am" had sent him to them. "I am" in Hebrew is *Eyah*, corresponding to the Akkadian *Ayah*.

The people in southern Mesopotamia knew of Yah, and some may even have seen him. But it was chiefly Adam whom God was working with, the reason being that God had an important plan for all humankind, which started with Adam who was first in the line to Christ.

---

1. *American Heritage Dictionary of the English Language*, 5th ed., s.v. "Ea." http://www.thefreedictionary.com/Ea. For an audio pronunciation of the word, click the speaker icon beside E·a, Babylonian god.

Chapter 12

Yahweh's Footsteps

God created mankind upright, but they have gone in search of many schemes.

—ECCL 7:29

ORIGINALLY YAHWEH SPOKE WITH men, and helped and advised them. The early chapters of Genesis fit well with what we know from science and archaeology. Genesis chapter 1 informs us that humans were hunter-gatherers (Paleolithic Period) who followed the animals and ate from what naturally grew in the ground or from trees. They were under an edict from God to "fill the earth, and subdue it," which they did because we can see the evidence they left behind. Genesis chapter 2 informs us about humans settling down and learning how to cultivate crops (Neolithic Period). The area where much of this agriculture took place was called the Fertile Crescent. The Lord God helped with some of the planting: in southern Mesopotamia he planted a garden. But men followed their own paths, as depicted well in the garden of Eden. And God cannot look upon sin. Habakkuk 1:13 (nasb) says, "Your eyes are too pure to approve evil, And You can not look on wickedness with favor." Evil is not a part of his nature and he cannot look on regardless. So he withdrew, but he did not leave us without hope. He breathed into Adam's line and fashioned Abraham's family all the way to Christ's birth.

We ought not to think it strange that God walked on earth and had fellowship with early humans. Jesus taught us that he was God's Son, and sons exhibit the inherited characteristics of their fathers. Jesus dwelt on earth for a time, walking around in a body. God is Spirit, but should he desire, he also was able to walk around in a like manner to Jesus. We sometimes say, "Like father like son," and Jesus himself said, the Son "can only do what he sees the Father doing, because whatever the Father does the Son also does" (John 5:19). The early days of humankind have some mystery around them: Isaiah 41:22 says, "Tell us what the former things were, so that we may consider them." A picture begins to emerge as we understand the Scriptures from their beginning to their ending—God uses the material world as a classroom from which we can all learn. "For since the creation of the world God's invisible qualities—his eternal power and divine nature—have been clearly seen, being understood from what has been made" (Rom 1:20). God uses the material world to teach us about the immaterial world. "We fix our eyes not on what is seen, but on what is unseen, since what is seen is temporary, but what is unseen is eternal" (2 Cor 4:18).

Yahweh had long since ceased appearing in a physical way when his Son was born of Mary. In a similar way, Jesus said he had to leave before the Holy Spirit would come: "It is for your good that I am going away. Unless I go away, the Advocate will not come to you" (John 16:7). The early books of the Bible present us with a picture of Yahweh being physically active in the primeval days of humankind, helping, advising, and supporting humanity in its infancy. Jesus told parables about "a man" who planted or built something but then had to leave to go on a long journey, such as in Luke 20:9: "A man planted a vineyard and rented it out to vine-growers, and went on a journey for a long time." Or Matthew 21:33: "There was a landowner who planted a vineyard. He put a wall around it, dug a winepress in it and built a watchtower. Then he rented the vineyard to some farmers and moved to another place." The man is Yahweh, and he did plant an actual garden and then left to go on a journey to another place. Jesus explained that Yahweh was here at one time on planet earth but left. Matthew 21:37 says, "Last of all, he sent his son to them. 'They will respect my son,' he said." The Father sent his Son, both Father and Son walked around on the earth: the Father, Yahweh, in southern Mesopotamia and later in Canaan, and the Son, Jesus, in Israel. Father and Son walked on earth just as a human father and son walk on earth.

Who has established all the ends of the earth? What is his name, and what is the name of his son? This is the question we are asked in Proverbs 30:4, and thanks to the Hebrew Old Testament and the Greek New

Testament we can answer those questions. Our heavenly Father came down to earth walking and speaking to men. He had a Son, and his Son was also found walking and speaking to men. Yahweh is our heavenly Father, his Son, Jesus was born into the human race, he is our brother. "Whatever you did for one of the least of these brothers and sisters of mine, you did for me" (Matt 25:40). "Jesus is not ashamed to call them brothers" (Heb 2:11 isv).

Men drew away from Yahweh, and followed their own selfish ideals and sinful pursuits. Yahweh withdrew from men. Jesus reconciles us to the Father through his own blood that paid the price of the debt to Yahweh that humankind found themselves in.

The particulars of how Yahweh walked on earth in the earlier times of humanity are not as well documented as when Yahweh's Son, Jesus walked on the earth, but there is enough information written down for us to understand that it did happen. Moses would later encourage the Israelites to look into their past. "Remember the days of old; consider the generations long past. Ask your father and he will tell you, your elders, and they will explain to you" (Deut 32:7). And the elders explained that back in Shinar (Sumer) before the Flood Yahweh looked after the line that would lead to Jacob. Angels looked after the other children of Adam, which may be where we get the Mesopotamian stories of each Sumerian city-state having its own god. The Septuagint reports in Deuteronomy 32:8–9, "he separated the sons of Adam, he set the bounds of the nations according to the number of the angels of God. And his people Jacob became the portion of the Lord, Israel was the line of his inheritance." Yahweh was active in Sumer/Shinar, which is referred to as being eastward (Gen 11:2).

Interestingly, in the ancient book of Job, we hear that Job was the greatest man among all the people of the east. We then get to read that there came a day when the angels presented themselves before Yahweh. I've heard people presume that the storyline suddenly takes us into heaven at that point, but we don't read that in the text. And furthermore, the writer of Job would also have to be translated into heaven to see this assembly of angels, but we don't read that anyone—the author, the angels, or Yahweh— were in heaven at that point. If certain angels each had their own group of Adam's children to look after in their own particular cities, then it makes sense that the angels presented themselves before Yahweh here on earth, and most likely in Sumer where Yahweh himself was looking after the line of Adam's offspring who would lead to Yahweh's Son being born.

Yahweh was based in and around the Edin area (as it was known by the Sumerians), similar to Jesus who was based in and around the country of Israel. Cain and Abel brought Yahweh offerings, indicating that he was approachable. And the book of Job picks up on that fact. We know Job is a very old book, and the narrative has a Mesopotamian feel as we read it. The book of Job presents us with a similar scenario to that found in the book of Genesis, namely, that Yahweh's footsteps were heard and his space-time frame was seen. Yahweh is able to appear, just as the angels are able to appear: they look like men but are not human men. Yahweh's body may have been of the same substance as Jesus's body after he had been resurrected.

As the biological chain of life progressed forward, each stage in the process built on what had gone before. God took care and time to sculpt life, first in the lower animals, then as life advanced, the higher animals kept what the lower animals had but their biological frame included improvements, and sometimes huge developments that enabled them to accomplish far more than their predecessors, until finally God crafted humans. Yahweh was not of human stock, of course, "it is He who made and us not we ourselves" (Ps 100:3 nasb). However, Jesus was born into a human family, and because of that he is able to lift the human race higher. Yahweh could be seen because he moved in the material universe; he had a body to do so. But he was not a part of the human race, though his Son did become a part of the human race.

Some people are not happy with the word "evolution," because there has been so much arguing about it and now it leaves a worried look on people's faces when they hear it. But we ought not to be afraid of it, because life has been moving ever higher. When Jesus took on his transformed body in the resurrection, "life" reached its peak. Through Christ, life has evolved into what it has been aiming at ever since the creation of the first smallest biological life form. Furthermore, because Jesus was human, what he has obtained, we can all obtain. Jesus "will transform our lowly bodies so that they will be like his glorious body" (Phil 3:21).

But let us remember that God is Spirit, which is the essence of his being. That's why no man can see God. Spirit is not seen with the human eye. Yahweh walked and talked with men because he was reaching out to us. He wants a relationship with us, and a part of the reaching out process meant he took on a form we can relate to. "All day long I have held out my hands to an obstinate people, who walk in ways not good, pursuing their own imaginations" (Isa 65:2). If we want to obtain the body that Jesus had in his resurrection, we need God's Spirit in us, because Jesus had God's Spirit. He was filled with the Holy Spirit: "Jesus, full of the Holy Spirit" (Luke 4:1). Each human being's goal is to be like Christ, that's where our life should be heading—towards the same body that Christ had in his resurrection. The apostle Paul said he wanted to know Christ and the power of his resurrection and somehow, himself to attain to the resurrection from the dead (Phil 3:10–11).

To meet the criteria for Christ's resurrected body, we must, like Paul, "know Christ," we must have God's Spirit in our lives. If we fail to respond to the "higher calling" that humans are invited to partake in, then we fail to reach the potential "life" was made for. As wonderful as organic life is, God's intention for us is higher still. We can exercise and eat the correct food and have a marvelous biological body, but if that's all we have, we fall short of the mark set for us.

God's Son bowed down and took on human form, now we humans need to bow down and humble ourselves and take on Christ's form. To take on God's Spirit and obtain the body the resurrected Christ has, means evolution will have reached its objective.

The body Christ had following his resurrection charted the same course that evolution follows, in which higher forms of life generally take on the characteristics of their predecessors but greater quality is added. So it was with Christ, after the resurrection. The disciples were struggling to come to terms with the resurrection, thinking that Jesus might even be a ghost. So Jesus said to them, "'Why are you troubled, and why do doubts rise in your minds? Look at my hands and my feet. It is I myself! Touch me and see; a ghost does not have flesh and bones, as you see I have.' And while they still did not believe it because of joy and amazement, he asked them, 'Do you have anything here to eat?' They gave him a piece of broiled fish, and he took it and ate it in their presence" (Luke 24:37–43). We see that the resurrected body of Christ could take part in the normal activities of life that we all do, but could also avoid normal restrictions like walls or gravity, and most importantly, death. His physical abilities were able to encompass all he had previously been able to do before the resurrection but now there were wonderful additions.

When Yahweh walked on earth, he also would have the extra attributes that his resurrected Son had. When Yahweh closed the door on the ark, he didn't have to run for it and get to safety, no, he was able to do the same as Christ did when eating supper with the two disciples he met on the road to Emmaus: "he disappeared from their sight" (Luke 24:31). We read twice in Genesis that "God went up," once before Abraham (Gen 17:22) and once before Jacob (Gen 35:13). Christ also went up as he ascended to heaven.

Chapter 13

A Turning Point In History

Now, here with Moses, standing before the burning bush, the era of Yahweh walking around on earth is more or less over. A new revelation of God is beginning to take place, and with this advent we humans were beginning to grasp a finer, more-detailed depiction of who God is, and Moses was the first person to experience this new disclosure.

Moses hid his face when he realized who was addressing him. Jacob had earlier exclaimed in fear, "How awesome is this place," when he woke from the dream of the ladder reaching heaven. Moses may have had similar feelings, but also in addition to the dreadful numinous quality of this encounter, he may have felt the added weight of being a sinful man in the presence of a good God.

The Lord got down to business, telling Moses he had seen and heard the misery of his people and that he was concerned for them. So he had come down to rescue them from the hand of the Egyptians. And furthermore, God was going to lead them out and take them to a specific location that was a good and spacious land, flowing with milk and honey. God even named the six people groups who were then occupying the precise location he was talking about (Exod 3:8).

Up to this point Moses was probably thinking, *All this sounds very good Lord. In fact, once, I did try to rescue the Israelites from the hand of the Egyptians myself, but it didn't work out well. But I'm glad that you are now on the case, you will undoubtedly have more success than me.* Then God said,

"So now, go. I am sending you to Pharaoh to bring my people the Israelites out of Egypt" (Exod 3:10). This last statement shook Moses.

Moses had heard about God, probably from his real mother, Jochabed. Moses had also been under the influence of Reuel who was a priest of God. Furthermore, he would be well acquainted with the gods spoken of by the Egyptians, from which there were many to choose. At this point God had not yet introduced himself to Moses as the God of heaven and earth but simply as the God of Abraham, Isaac, and Jacob. Moses was on a learning curve himself. Since his last attempt at being a hero ended in shambles, Moses had been humbled and was now quite content to spend his days with Jethro's family around him in Midian, he didn't want any excitement of this nature in his life. So Moses, feeling cornered by the God of Abraham, Isaac, and Jacob needs to think on his feet and he reasons that God's directive warrants a response, so he ventures a reply. "Who am I that I should go to Pharaoh?" (Exod 3:11). Moses was right, who was he? He'd lost all privileges of being in the royal court, in fact he was a wanted man in Egypt, although the pharaoh who issued the judgement was now dead and a new pharaoh was in place.

Amenhotep II had been born about 5 years after Moses's escape to Midian, so the pharaoh now in charge would not know Moses. Moses was living long, and his features would probably have changed a little with age. His appearance would also be different from being a clean-shaven regal Egyptian to a shepherd with the likeness of a shepherd. Owing to his long life and image change, if there were some people in Egypt who may remember him from his days in the Egyptian royalty, he may still be able to move freely without revealing who he actually was. But Moses would hear the skeleton in his closet rattling quite loudly.

Another worrying feature for Moses of this request from God would be that Moses had heard about the new pharaoh's character. The *Encyclopaedia Britannica* advises us that Amenhotep II's warrior father carefully guided his upbringing, with great emphasis on physical strength, skills of warfare, and sportsmanship. Amenhotep II never tired of boasting of his feats in these skills. We've already heard of Amenhotep II's disdain for foreigners, and Moses would have heard these things too.

God replies by telling Moses that he will be with him, and that once the Israelites are out of Egypt they will worship God on this mountain—Mount Horeb. That must have sounded a little strange to Moses, because he knew that the area God had previously been describing to him, the land of the Canaanites, Hittites, Amorites, Perizzites, Hivites, and Jebusites was northwards, a long way north from where Moses was on Mount Horeb. Why would the Israelites head south into the Sinai Peninsula?

Moses, still quite disturbed by the instruction to confront pharaoh, tried another angle of remonstration: "Suppose I go to the Israelites and say to them, 'The God of your fathers has sent me to you,' and they ask me, 'What is his name?' Then what shall I tell them?" (Exod 3:13).

Moses had asked a clever question. There were beliefs in ancient Egypt that once you knew someone's name you had some sort of hold over them. Occasionally, we still see it today; people, for various reasons, are unwilling to give their name to someone. They may even say, "Why do you want to know my name?"

The Egyptians had a famous myth about the goddess Isis, who discovered the sun god Ra's secret name. Once she knew Ra's name she increased her powers. A name was more than a simple label used to identify someone: something of the god's or person's nature was revealed in the name. The particular way in which Isis is said to have gained knowledge of Ra's name was by making a snake that looked like a spear. She placed the snake on the pathway that Ra usually took. The snake bit Ra and in his pain he asked Isis to relieve his suffering, she promised to do this but only if Ra told her his name. He did his best to resist Isis's offer and even tried to palm Isis off with a speech that sounded like he was revealing his name, but he actually wasn't. Isis was too clever for him and soon realized that Ra's fine-sounding words didn't actually reveal his name. Eventually the pain became too intense for Ra and he gave in and surrendered his name. Once Ra had given Isis his name he could not take back that knowledge from her, and she in turn was made even stronger by the information Ra had imparted to her.

So that's a little background on the kind of religion Moses may have been brought up with in the family of Hatshepsut. And with Moses not being familiar with the God of Abraham, Isaac, and Jacob, he may have thought this God would be not unlike the gods he had heard stories of in Egypt. After all, most of the gods' whims and characters are similar aren't they? The phrase that people sometimes say, "It's in the lap of the gods," reveals a little of what humans tend to think of the pantheon of gods. The myths that come down to us, inform us that gods can be pedantic, secretive, jealous, and scheming.

But Moses was in for another surprise, because the God of Abraham, Isaac, and Jacob was not at all like the gods he had heard about in Egypt.

In fact the God before him now, in the burning bush, was quite happy to reveal his name without any reservations at all. Abraham's family already knew the name of Yahweh, but now the Lord not only allows Moses to know his name but also begins to explain in detail what his name means.

Moses had previously said to the Lord, "Who am I?" But now God, in his glory, changes Moses's insipid statement around and pronounces the awe inspiring, "I am who I am" (Exod 3:14). The world had never heard this before. It was new—the self-existent one, self-sufficient, needing no material apparatus to support his being. He is.

Sometimes some people wonder why the Bible begins with "In the beginning God." Why is there no explanation of how God got there in the first place? Why is there no account of where God came from? Sometimes people ask, "Who made God?" Professor of Mathematics at Oxford University, John Lennox, informs us that when skeptical people ask us to tell them where God came from, it does prove one thing—"If they had a better argument they would use it."[1]

A created God would not be God.

Tell the Israelites: "I AM sent me to you." (Exod 3:14 isv)

We saw in the book of Genesis that the Lord makes good use of interconnecting poetic wordplay, and we see a similar utilization of that with the divine name. "I am who I am" is first person, God changes that around to the third person with the word, "Yahweh"—"He is"—but the meaning is the same. "God is." "This is my name forever" (Exod. 3:15), God said to Moses. We see that when the Lord told Moses to reach out to the Israelites, he also equipped him with some astounding instruction for them on God's very nature.

"I am"—the Mesopotamian *Ayah* would resonate with the Israelites because Abraham, who was from Mesopotamia, would have known this name well, and passed the information on to his offspring. When Genesis 4:26 tells us that men began to call on the name of the LORD, the Hebrew text for "LORD" is "Yahweh." This, of course, is a long time before Moses met Yahweh in the burning bush. So we see that the generations of men prior to Moses knew the name of Yahweh, or at least the contracted version of the name: Yah. Some modern theologians wonder if men, including Abraham, exclusively used the name Yah, and not Yahweh before the time of Moses. If that is so the reason we find the name Yahweh in the book

1. Lennox, *God's Undertaker*, 182.

of Genesis is that Moses used the name Yahweh retrospectively when he compiled the text of Genesis.

Moses's dialogue with God at the burning bush was not going the way Moses wanted, he was desperately looking for a "get out" clause, but had so far failed to find one. God then begins to outline the plan of Israel's escape from Egypt in some detail. God knows Pharaoh, and knew an effective strategy to tackle the situation, so at first, all Moses has to do is represent the Israelite workforce as a trade union leader might and request a holiday for the workers at a location three days' journey away. But Moses is still very unsettled by this whole matter and his next line of defense is: in all likelihood the Israelites would not believe him. After all, Moses had some history in trying to persuade his fellow Israelites to fall into line with him. God's response to this problem is to give Moses a tool to use, and he asks Moses, "What is that in your hand?" (Exod 4:2). Moses used a staff to keep the animals in line, and he had it with him. Then the Lord told Moses to throw the staff on the ground and when he did so, the rod transformed into a snake, which alarmed Moses and he ran. This encounter at the bush not only had its dreadful aspect but, with the appearance of the snake, there was physical fear too. When Moses wrote this down, he remembered the little quirk of actually running from the snake because this event was burned into his memory—there was no one else around, so it was up to Moses to record the events.

There may be a little more to the stick and snake episode than meets the eye. The story of the goddess Isis using a snake that looked like a spear may have been in the mind of Moses when he asked the Lord his name. The myth is now turned around and God shows Moses his ability to surpass the Egyptian gods. When Moses takes the snake by the tail, which must have required some bravery, the snake turned back into a stick.

Normally, the miracles of Jesus followed the pattern laid down by nature using a process of speeding up the natural laws. Water turning into wine for example, which God the Father does through nature all the time, using rain and vines. Or bread into more bread (feeding of the 4,000 and 5,000), farmers plant the seeds of wheat, which are multiplied into much more wheat in the ground as they grow. But Moses saw an extraordinary miracle (if it's possible to describe a miracle as ordinary in the first place).

The structure of a stick and a snake are not necessarily too different. All living organisms share the DNA double helix, so a stick becoming a snake means a fast alteration of the DNA code within each organism. God, through this miracle, does not necessarily break the faithfulness of the laws he set down for the physics of the universe, but works within them. Evolution works in a slow way to sculpt organisms into what God intends for them. With this miracle we see an accelerating process, as we often do with miracles in the Bible.

God has made physical laws and he does use them. The laws and principles we see in creation are still around us today. For instance we could say, "Why does God need to have 100 million sperm to fertilize one egg in a woman's fallopian tube?" God could do it with one sperm if he wanted to. Yes, he could, but he has chosen to use the principal of probability, or what is known as the law of large numbers, it's what a layman calls the law of averages. Or we could say, "Why does it rain on the sea?" It is the land that needs the rain not the sea. But that's the way God has designed the universe, things have a way of working out well using the law of large numbers. But God doesn't have to use that law if there is a reason not to. He is able to speed up the process and change DNA code for what we know as a miracle. A "genome" is all of a living organism's genetic material, the entire set of instructions that make each person what they are. Each human being has a unique genome, so in the resurrection of the dead we will see a speeding up process of each person's unique code being assembled because God knows what each person's genetic code is. He also knows the code of a snake and a stick.

Moses's protestations had failed again. Furthermore, God pressed his point by giving Moses a second sign where Moses was told to place his hand into his cloak and when he withdrew it his hand was leprous like snow. This is interesting because the Egyptian historian Manetho, writing in the 3rd century BC, tells one story where he depicts a man named Osarseph as a renegade Egyptian priest who leads an army of lepers and other unclean people against a pharaoh named Amenophis. They commit many sacrileges against the gods, before the pharaoh expels them. Towards the end of the story Osarseph changes his name to Moses. The whole story is more complicated and we don't have any copies of Manetho's record but other early historian writers do quote him, which is where we get the story. The account may have been mashed up a little but the interesting part is that if Moses used the sign of his leprous hand, then it's possible that his followers would also be called lepers along with him.

Moses was able to get his hand restored by placing it again into his cloak and on its withdrawal the hand was back to normal. We see another speeding up process, for a man's hand could naturally become leprous over a period of time. There is also a warning and a lesson attached: what happened to Moses could happen to others. Sometime later when Miriam, the sister of Moses, complained about Moses and his Ethiopian wife, enabling Miriam to set herself up against Moses, God judged between them and when the cloud of the Lord lifted, Miriam was white with leprosy. Moses cried out to the Lord, "Please, God, heal her!" She was healed but she had to stay outside the camp for 7 days.

Then the Lord said,

> If they do not believe you or pay attention to the first sign, they may believe the second. But if they do not believe these two signs or listen to you, take some water from the Nile and pour it on the dry ground. The water you take from the river will become blood on the ground. (Exod 4:8–9)

So Moses had three signs at his disposal, surely he would now feel able to accomplish the task laid out for him. But no!

Moses's next reply begins with "Oh Lord." We can sense the pleading tone with the first two words. Moses goes on to report that he is not very good with words. He never has been, and he's not now, even though God has spoken to him he gets tongue-tied, and his words get tangled.

Moses does not want to do this job of work, but God has invested too much in Moses to let him wriggle out of it. The Lord met each reply from Moses with a reasoned response that would help him. The fact is, in God's eyes, Moses was the man for this job. His childhood, education, military experience, and his years as a shepherd all went towards helping him lead the people of Israel out of Egypt. Then there was also Moses's skill as a writer, he was able to write legislation and leave a record of events that we are thinking about at this moment.

> Who gave human beings their mouths? Who makes them deaf or mute? Who gives them sight or makes them blind? Is it not I, the Lord? So now go, and I will be with your mouth and will teach you what you must say. (Exod 4:11–12)

When Abraham spoke with Yahweh about saving his relative Lot, he whittled down the number of righteous men from 50 to 10 and the Lord listened patiently while Abraham got to his point (Gen 18:22–33). Abraham showed respect by saying, "Now that I have been so bold as to speak to the Lord, though I am nothing but dust and ashes." Or "May the Lord not be angry, but let me speak." Abraham did have a history with Yahweh that Moses did not have, and we can see Abraham's reverence to whom he was speaking. Moses speaks to the Lord in a different way, but still God is patient, polite, and takes each objection seriously with an appropriate response.

Moses, now devoid of any reasonable objection to excuse himself from the task, tries one last ditch attempt to get off the divine hook by crying out, "O Lord, please send someone else to do it" (Exod 4:13).

God's response to this last plea was said forcefully, but still with a reasonable explanation. "What about your brother, Aaron the Levite? I know he can speak well. He is already on his way to meet you, and he will be glad to see you" (Exod 4:14).

This scenario lends itself to Aaron being one of the workers assigned to the latest expedition heading to the mining works at Serabit el-Khadim—we know Aaron was good at casting metal. Surprisingly, or rather we should say, "providentially," Aaron was on his way at that very moment. God knew all this of course, and had scheduled it into his plans. Whether Moses knew Aaron was one of the workers, we can't be sure. Perhaps he did know or thought it was a possibility and so volunteered himself to Jethro for the job of taking the flocks to Serabit el-Khadim. However, it is more probable that Moses did not know Aaron was on his way because the Lord conveyed to Moses that his brother Aaron would be glad to see him, which seems to suggest the two brothers hadn't seen each other for a long time and that Moses wasn't aware that his brother was on the way.

Shortly after Moses encountered Yahweh at Mount Horeb, Aaron arrived and Moses made himself known to his brother. Aaron may have replied,

"Moses, my brother, what joy fills my heart to see you. What brings you to this mine?"

"I have delivered a consignment of animals to your 'Keeper of Supplies.' You will be feasting on my sheep and goats, for the next few weeks brother. But listen, we must talk, something wonderful and most dreadful has occurred. I am still shaking in my sandals."

So, Moses told his brother what had happened to him and what the plan of action would be.

First, Moses needed to travel the 116 miles back to Midian. The return journey would take less time now that the herd had been dispensed with. Once back home in Midian, Moses does not appear to take on his task as an Israelite delegate readily, there was some delay, probably because of his fear of those who were waiting to kill him back in Egypt. Moses had put up so many arguments with the Lord back at the burning bush because Egypt had some extremely powerful men after his very life, so his reluctance to go back to Egypt makes sense. We can picture Moses with Jethro's family trying hard to settle back into life as he knew it, but frequently looking over his shoulder for the "I am," wondering if some nearby bush may burst into flames. We can also see the gracious behavior of the Lord, patiently waiting, and bearing with his chosen spokesperson until Moses felt he was ready. Moses needed a nudge, so God gave him one. How it happened we are not told but the Lord spoke to Moses again, back in Midian, and he was told to get his act together.

Moses was not going to escape the God of Abraham, Isaac, and Jacob that easily. The Lord reassured Moses that all the men who wanted to kill him were dead. So, finally, Moses approached Jethro, the head of his adopted tribe, to ask permission to go to Egypt and check on his family there. Which was truthful, but Moses thought it best not to disclose the higher calling that he had been assigned, at least at this stage. Jethro would not want to see Moses go, but agreed with a good heart.

By this time Moses had two sons, Gershom and Eliezer, so along with his wife they started out for Egypt. They took a donkey to help with the travelling. He also took the staff, which he didn't really need for sheep this time, but it was needed as a tool to use before the Israelites and then for Pharaoh.

Chapter 14

At War With Yahweh

THE CITY OF NEKHEL is halfway between Midian and Egypt. Moses and his close family would have travelled about 70 miles when they stopped at a resting place, most likely at Nekhel.

The next incident that happens is one of those hard-to-understand scenarios, similar to when Jacob wrestled with a man in the book of Genesis. But if we look at the picture presented in the book of Exodus we should be able to piece together what happened. The text says,

> At a lodging place on the way, the LORD met Moses and was about to kill him. But Zipporah took a flint knife, cut off her son's foreskin and touched Moses's feet with it. "Surely you are a bridegroom of blood to me," she said. So the LORD let him alone. (Exod 4:24–25)

Moses was three months old when he was placed into the basket on the Nile, which means he would have already been circumcised, because Hebrew babies were circumcised on the eighth day, as Abraham did with Isaac. So God was quite happy to work with Moses because he conformed to the covenant agreement that God had made with Abraham.

> This is my covenant with you and your descendants after you, the covenant you are to keep: Every male among you shall be circumcised. (Gen 17:10)

Moses had been talking to the Lord, which was fine because Moses was circumcised. However, now Moses had commenced the great task he was commissioned with and he had brought along with him at least one male who was not circumcised, and that changed things dramatically. There was an important covenant in place and God does not break covenant, he is faithful to his promise to Abraham. Moses didn't have the time spent with his fellow Israelites to learn about the importance of circumcision, but nevertheless may have mentioned it to Zipporah soon after their sons were born. Zipporah may have not liked the idea, and Moses may not have felt strongly enough about the practice to pursue the matter. But now Moses had travelled a long way on foot and he appears to have picked up an infection that has affected his feet. He could have trod on something sharp and the cut got infected, and now he was unwell, and so weakened by it that he was close to death.

Over these last few months Moses had been getting to know the Lord and something told him the Lord was using this infection, and Moses was pretty sure he knew the reason. Moses explained his reasoning to his wife who may have thought otherwise. So Moses implored Zipporah to circumcise their son, as by now he was too weak to do it himself. Zipporah, still not happy with the proceedings, reluctantly gets on with the operation and then touches his feet with the foreskin. Moses makes a good recovery.

Immediately after the circumcision of the son of Moses and Zipporah, the next story we are told takes us back to Aaron's point of view before he first went to Serabit el-Khadim.

> Now the LORD said to Aaron, "Go to meet Moses in the wilderness." So he went and met him at the mountain of God and kissed him. (Exod 4:27)

We know the text is taking us back to a time before Moses met God at the burning bush for two reasons. Firstly, the Hebrew language used in the Old Testament is not able to use the pluperfect tense. The pluperfect tense is used when referring to something that occurred earlier than the time being considered, when the time being considered is already in the past. So, in order to prepare the readers for something that is about to be told, the writer feels obliged to go back and to detail what had taken place prior to the stage at which his narrative has arrived. So, we understand that God had "earlier" told Aaron to make his way to Serabit el-Khadim. Accordingly, Aaron volunteered himself for the work of the next expedition to the mine at Serabit el-Khadim. Aaron was under strict Egyptian rule and therefore would not have been able to get away to the area 170 miles away unless he attached himself to the mining workforce.

Secondly, we also know we've gone back to an earlier point in the story to see events from Aaron's perspective because the route Moses and his family were now taking from Midian to Egypt is nowhere near the mountain where God met Moses. So we conclude that verses 27 and 28 of chapter 4 of Exodus are a parenthesis explaining previous events from Aaron's perspective so that we can understand what follows from verse 29 to the end of the chapter.

Moses made his way to Egypt and sought out his brother Aaron, who by this time had completed the work he was assigned at the Serabit el-Khadim smelting works. Then the two brothers gathered together the elders of the Israelite community. We need to remember that Jacob's family had continued to increase in number and were spread out somewhat since they first settled in the land of Egypt. Once the representative Israelites had been assembled, Moses used his staff to perform the staff-to-snake wonder, and along with two other signs the Israelite elders were quick to believe. They had been crying out for a long time under their oppression so to hear that the God of their fathers was now taking up their case was very good news. They then worshipped the Lord as a community in true humility. Oppression does have a way of breaking us down, and God will use the adverse circumstances in our lives to sculpt us into the people we ought to be.

Pharaoh Amenhotep II was based in Memphis, which is in Lower Egypt about 75 miles from Goshen. There were also royal palatial premises at Avaris, which was a lot closer to Goshen. Psalm 78, verses 12 and 43 mention the field of Zoan as the region where Moses displayed his wonders before the Israelites. If, at that time, Amenhotep II was based in Avaris, Moses and Aaron would have a 13-mile journey south from the field of Zoan (which is near the modern town of San Al Hagar).

An audience with Pharaoh Amenhotep II was arranged, and he was willing to meet the representatives of the Israelite workforce. The Israelites probably occupied a small part of Pharaoh's thoughts, as Egypt was a long country, over 900 miles in length, with a population of around 4.5 million people. He also had a building program, military campaigns, as well as regular domestic affairs, so although the Israelites were a small part of his overall awareness of what was happening during his reign, they were still a useful resource towards his many projects, so he would want to keep them in place.

The first meeting did not go well. Amenhotep II, as we know, was not slow to make his feelings known. Essentially saying:

"What's this talk about taking the people away from their work? Who is Yahweh, that I should obey him? I do not know Yahweh and I will not let Israel go."

Declaring war with Yahweh is not a good idea; he is always one step ahead. But Pharaoh was so incensed at this request that that same day he rushed through orders to increase the workload of the Israelites. The supply of straw for their brick making industry would be withdrawn. The orders were to be strictly adhered to—if a particular crew of Israelite workmen failed to achieve their quota for the day their Israelite foreman would face the penalty of being beaten.

The Israelite foremen themselves requested a royal audience, to find out why the supply of straw had been withdrawn. The pharaoh was still infuriated and insults the foremen in a sarcastic dismissive manner, labeling them "lazy."

Moses and Aaron would be well aware of the foremen's meeting with Pharaoh and were waiting outside the palace grounds to meet the foremen and see how the meeting went. The Israelite leaders let their frustration out on Moses and Aaron for putting them into this position. The foremen said, "May Yahweh look upon you and judge" (Exod 5:21). Moses had no reply for the supervisors because he was as dismayed as they were. Moses in turn went to the Lord.

Jesus taught us to retreat to a private place: "When you pray, go into your room, close the door and pray to your Father" (Matt 6:6). Since Moses first met the Lord at the burning bush, God had been close to him. He would find some solitary place and cry out to the Lord. Moses himself wanted to know why Yahweh had brought trouble upon these people, citing the name of Yahweh as the beginning of the present trouble.

> Ever since I went to Pharaoh to speak in your name, he has brought trouble on this people, and you have not rescued your people at all. (Exod 5:23)

Yahweh explains to Moses that it had to be that way. We can now see that God was doing something special at that time in Egypt, and was showing a new aspect of his being and power to the world. What God was doing through Moses, Pharaoh, and the Israelites would be remembered throughout the ages to follow. The procedure was a protracted process, not a quick fix, so Moses and the Israelites needed faith. But the Israelites' faith was at a low point. So God points out to Moses that Abraham, Isaac, and Jacob had known him up to a point, but now he was doing something new.

The patriarchs had not known him to work in this way or seen what Moses had seen in the burning bush.

God also said to Moses,

> I am the Lord. I appeared to Abraham, to Isaac and to Jacob as God Almighty, (El Shaddai) but by my name Yahweh I did not make myself fully known to them. (Exod 6:2–3)

"El" is singular for God, "Elohim" is the plural for El. There are a number of ways people look at the word Elohim but it may help us if we remember that the Bible begins by saying, "In the beginning God (Elohim) created the heavens and the earth." That does not mean there is more than one God who created the universe, Elohim is used in a similar way to which we might use the word "human." For instance we could say, "The telephone is a human invention," which it is, but it was invented by one particular human, Alexander Graham Bell. Some Bible versions occasionally translate the word "elohim" as angels: Psalm 8:4–5 says, "What is mankind that you are mindful of them, human beings that you care for them? You have made them a little lower than the angels. (elohim)." When Jethro speaks with Moses a little later in the book of Exodus he says, "Now I know that the LORD (Yahweh) is greater than all other gods (elohim)" (Exod 18:11).

The Bible lets us know that angels can be seraphim (Isa 6:2) or cherubim (Gen 3:24). People also talk of ophanim, which they identify with the beings Ezekiel saw, or the "thrones" Paul talks about in Colossians 1:16. But certainly, according to the Bible God has created other beings of which we only know a little. The singular of "seraphim" is "seraph" and "cherub" is singular for "cherubim." The Bible tells us that angels have been on earth at various times for various reasons. They can appear as men, not human men, but men in as much as they have a material body. And in the early days of human civilization, angelic beings helped humankind as Deuteronomy 32:7–8 (Septuagint) points out: "When the Most High divided the nations, when he separated the sons of Adam, he set the bounds of the nations according to the number of the angels of God." (The Masoretic text differs on this reading, but the Septuagint and Dead Sea Scrolls have the earlier reading.) Angels looked after Adam's dispersing family members. Some of the angels fell from the purity in which they were created. Men also fell, and some men worshipped angels. So the angelic beings were thought of as elohim too, which is where false gods come into play. However, God (El), of course, is stronger than any false elohim. When God is called El-Shaddai,

Shaddai's primary meaning is "strong so as to overpower."[1] So although God walked on earth too, with Adam, Abel, Noah, Enoch, and Abraham he allowed men to think of him as Elohim but an Elohim who is stronger than any other elohim. And of course God is strong so as to overpower any false elohim.

God was teaching Moses about the nature of Yahweh. The essence of his being is not material. He is Spirit, we cannot see spirit, but everything we can see was made by he who is unseen. So what is unseen is immeasurably more important than what can be seen. Could Moses grasp this? God's revelation of himself to humans was a gradual process until finally "in these last days he has spoken to us by his Son, whom he appointed heir of all things, and through whom also he made the universe" (Heb 1:2).

Abraham knew God as El-Shaddai, but there was far more revelation to come.

---

1. *Ellicott's Commentary For English Readers*, s.v. "Genesis 17:1" and "Exodus 6:3," para 1. http://biblehub.com/commentaries/genesis/17-1.htm.

Chapter 15

How to Harden a Heart

MOSES WENT BACK TO the Israelites and tried to explain what he had been told by Yahweh about God's nature. Moses also recounted what Yahweh had said about getting them out of Egypt and into the promised land. But the Israelites were in no mood to listen. Moses was in the position of being ignored by the people he was trying to help. He was merely a curiosity, and talk of promises made to their ancestors about going to Canaan were simply a pipe dream. Moses had their initial support but now that their hardships had increased any backing he may have received from them evaporated. Moses and Aaron were at a loss what to do next and would have been on their own if God had not been on their side.

The Lord then steps into the situation and tells Moses,

> Go, tell Pharaoh king of Egypt to let the Israelites go out of his country. (Exod 6:10–11)

But Moses is in such a state of despondency that we can almost hear a "Ha" at the beginning of his reply. The Living Bible puts it like this:

> "But look," Moses objected, "my own people won't even listen to me anymore; how can I expect Pharaoh to? I'm no orator!" (Exod 6:12)

Most of the rest of Exodus chapter 6 details the genealogical line that ends with Moses and Aaron, and points out that the two brothers were Israelites—bone of bone, and flesh of flesh of those whom they were sent to deliver—just as another deliverer would be many generations later.

The last two verses of Exodus chapter 6 pick up where the story had previously taken us. So in chapter 7 we're off again. The Lord highlights his plan of action to Moses. A second audience with Pharaoh is planned. How long all these proceedings took, must have moved into many months. Moses was now 80 years old and Aaron was 83. When they were first reunited, back at the mine of Serabit el-Khadim, 5 years or more could have elapsed.

For a second time, as God had asked them to do, Moses and Aaron stood before Pharaoh with words to the effect of, "Yahweh asks you to let the Israelites go out of Egypt." The Lord had primed Moses and Aaron so they knew that Pharaoh would have a request for them. We can imagine the dialogue that preceded Pharaoh's request quite well:

"I am Amenhotep II, king of Egypt. I was made the setem-priest of Lower Egypt while still a youth. Who is this Yahweh? Is he greater than the gods of Egypt? Greater than Amun or Ptah? What is Yahweh able to do? Show me something of his power? Perform for me a miracle."

The apostle Paul uses this particular pharaoh as an example of someone whose heart is hard. Paul uses the phrase, God has mercy on whom he wants to have mercy, and he hardens whom he wants to harden (Rom 9:18). So how did God harden Pharaoh's heart? We know each human is made in God's image, so therefore each human being has the ability to make decisions. We do not operate as automatons, God has made us individuals who can choose to respond to God's overtures of love towards us or not. However, God can see what we are made of, and he knows whether the core of someone's being is turned towards him or away from him. When certain people see someone in need they will not help, even if it is in their power to do so, because they only care about their own pleasure. We call this "selfishness." This self-centeredness can get to the stage where it sets itself up as a despotic god in people's lives. The living God warns us about the futility of having any other gods. God could see what Pharaoh had become. If we look at Pharaoh from God's perspective we may find he says something like this:

"Amenhotep II, I can see what you have become, you are not pleasing to me. I wish you were, but you have chosen to reject my ways and have become what you are. So therefore, as you have become a tyrant oppressing the Israelites, you will find out that your own god of selfishness is also a tyrant. Follow selfishness where you will, it will not lead you to freedom but slavery. I will also use your devotion to your god as an example to anyone who thinks that selfish behavior is a legitimate way forward for human beings who are made in my image."

In ancient Egypt magic was a big deal. There were magicians who specialized in awe-inspiring feats of magic that would fascinate people who thought they were witnessing supernatural events before their very eyes. The Bible, in a number of places, teaches us that God has made the world stable. (This is something I outlined in my book *Fishing for Praise*.) It is not given to men or angels to tamper with the infrastructure of the physical universe. Modern-day magicians are said to be honest people because they tell people they are going to fool them and then proceed to fool them, often quite amazingly. But in antiquity magicians were not always so honest and let people believe they were witnessing a suspension of the natural laws of physics.

God, of course, knew this, and knew in particular that there were a number of feats of skill by the magicians in ancient Egypt utilizing snakes. The Egyptians had quite an interest in snakes so the illusionists exploited people's curiosity and worked on perfecting tricks that involved snakes. Snakes can be put into some sort of hypnotic state, which makes them easier to work with. I have seen a video of a magic show where the magician performed the impressive trick of turning a cane into a snake, such were the illusions that were popular at that time in Egypt. We know this because when Aaron threw down the staff and it turned into a snake before Pharaoh, rather than believe Moses, Pharaoh called for his own magicians, who were able to replicate, through sleight-of-hand, an illusion of cane-into-snake that was close enough to convince him that Moses and Aaron were nothing special. God knew Pharaoh would want to see a wonder, and God graciously showed him a genuine miracle. Pharaoh either dismissed the supernatural work of God as a parlor trick or decided to take on Yahweh as an adversary—anything Yahweh can do my enchanters can also do.

"The magicians of Egypt, they also did in like manner with their enchantments" (Exod 7:11 kjv). The true meaning of the word *lĕhâtim*, translated "enchantments" in Exodus seems to be our modern-day phrase sleight of hand.[1]

Two of the most impressive magicians in Egypt at that time are named for us in 2 Timothy 3:8, and although their names are not found in the Old Testament, the names did, somehow, find their way into the New Testament era, perhaps through some manuscripts we no longer have or maybe oral tradition. Paul talks to Timothy about Jannes and Jambres, who stood against Moses, as if Timothy would be well aware who Jannes and Jambres

---

1. Rosenmüller, *Scholia in Vetus Testamentum*, 110.

were. If the snakes used by Pharaoh's two magicians had been hypnotized then the snake produced by the hand of God wouldn't find it hard to overcome the other two snakes, which happened as Exodus informs us.

Pharaoh had a chance to talk to Moses in a sincere way about God: he could have said, "Tell me more, I am a priest and want to know about all matters divine." When Herod the tetrarch had Jesus standing before him, he hoped Jesus would perform one of the miracles he'd heard about. But Jesus did not conform to Herod's wishes and remained silent (Luke 23:8–9). Pharaoh had been given much more than Herod. Moses was there as an emissary of the living God, but it meant Pharaoh had to lose some manual workers for a while and he was unwilling to do so. The desire of the pharaohs to build magnificent monuments and edifices greater than that of their predecessors was probably in Amenhotep II's mind, and he was not prepared to let go of his pride or any of his workforce. Over 400 years earlier, people in southern Mesopotamia said, "Come, let us build ourselves a city, with a tower that reaches to the heavens, so that we may make a name for ourselves" (Gen 11:4). Yahweh went down to see the city and tower. Men of power have a desire to "make a name" for themselves, and it seems that Pharaoh was in this position. All human beings have a similar choice to make, although the circumstances for each one of us may be different. We all have a get-out clause if we choose to look for one. God is after a humble heart, he is searching for those who will worship in spirit and truth (John 4:23). So yes, God hardened Pharaoh's heart, but we can just as easily say that God tried all means of softening Pharaoh's heart, even to the point of showing him a miracle. God provides the circumstantial material for each one of us to choose. Pharaoh chose to close his heart. Pharaoh did the choosing: God gave him the apparatus with which to choose and Pharaoh decided to harden his heart. Living with a hard heart is not what God intends for any one of us.

Chapter 16

River of Blood

MOSES AND AARON HAD sought out two official meetings with Pharaoh. The Israelite foremen had also requested an audience with the king to find out why their workload and subsequent punishments had been increased. Altogether three official royal meetings with Israelite representatives took place. By now Pharaoh was beginning to understand who the Israelites were, even though they may have occupied only a small part of his perception of Egypt as a whole. He was becoming familiar with who their leaders were and he also knew the God they belonged to was called Yahweh. Pharaoh had seen something spectacular and yet had chosen to stand hard against Yahweh by not giving the Israelites any freedom to go and hold a festival to their God. Pharaoh had had his fill of the bleating Hebrews and wanted to hear no more from them. Further official meetings with the pharaoh would not be easy to arrange.

The next meeting between Pharaoh and Moses was unofficial. The Lord knew exactly where Pharaoh would be, so arranging a meeting with Pharaoh as long as God is on your side is straightforward. God told Moses to wait on the bank of the river Nile in the morning as Pharaoh goes out to the water. We can presume that Pharaoh was near Zoan. Firstly, he went to the river for his morning wash rather than using vessels brought by servants in his palace. Normally the incumbent pharaoh would bathe in one of his private chapels. Pharaoh bathed his body each morning as the sun god Ra did in the ocean of the heavens. There was some symbolism attached to Pharaoh's morning bathing ritual.[1] Secondly, Zoan is the place near to where the Israelites' borders were encroaching northward. Thirdly, Psalm 78:43 tells us that this next phase of negotiations occurred in the field of Zoan.

Zoan is what the Greeks called Tanis and its popular historical name is also Tanis. The Egyptians later called the city Djanet, but the actual city of Djanet/Tanis wasn't built until 100 years or so after Amenhotep II. The area itself, before the city was built upon it, was well known by the earlier Egyptian dynasties as the Field of Dja'u, though the Israelites called it the field of Zoan.[2] The Bible in Psalm 78 mentions the field of Zoan twice as the area where Moses performed his miracles. The field of Dja'u was known in Egyptian antiquity as a good fishing and fowling preserve.

Perhaps Pharaoh Amenhotep II was in the area for a few days recreational fishing, fowling, and hunting. The palatial residence at Avaris was about 13 miles south of the field of Zoan, but a royal camp could have been set up if Amenhotep II particularly enjoyed the area. For whatever reason Amenhotep II was there, he was in for a surprise that particular morning.

Exodus 7:15–18 tells us that Moses made himself known to the pharaoh, probably by shouting something like this from the opposite riverbank:

> Yahweh, the God of the Hebrews, has sent me to say to you, "Let my people go, so that they may worship me in the wilderness." But until now you have not listened, so Yahweh says, "By this you will know that I am Yahweh": I will use the staff that is in my hand to strike the water of the Nile, and it will be changed into blood. The fish in the Nile will die, and the river will stink; the Egyptians will not be able to drink its water.

The field of Dja'u was a known fishing area, so it is noteworthy that the fish are singled out for a mention. This new phase of negotiations with Pharaoh ushers in the famous plagues of Egypt.

We have the plagues recorded for us in the book of Exodus, and they are also addressed in Psalm 78:44–51. The first, and shocking, plague is water being turned into blood. This was one of the miraculous signs that God first told Moses about at the burning bush. There is a well-known ancient Egyptian document, presently housed in the Netherlands at the Dutch National Museum of Antiquities, which speaks of the river being turned to blood. The manuscript is called the "The Admonitions of an Egyptian Sage" and known as the Ipuwer Papyrus because an Egyptian called Ipuwer

1. White, *Life*, 113.
2. Dunn, "Tanis (El-Hagar)," para. 6.

wrote it and it may provide an independent record of the plagues in Egypt. There is a fair amount of skepticism regarding these claims. Believers may think that God has left posterity an eyewitness account for the plagues that struck Egypt, and skeptics think that there may be some similarities, but the papyrus was probably written before the events described in the book of Exodus. The Ipuwer document in the museum is a copy and not the original, and there is reluctance to date when the original document was written. The neutral observer may be reluctant to conclude that the document has little to do with the plagues. The sole surviving manuscript dates to the later part of 1300s BC, so the original would be earlier. The plagues as told in the book of Exodus occurred around 1407 or 1406 BC. The Ipuwer Papyrus says, "Indeed, the river is blood, yet men drink of it. Men shrink from human beings and thirst after water."[3]

When we hear about the first plague we immediately find ourselves thinking, *What? Real blood? You mean like O Rhesus Positive or A Rhesus Negative type of blood?*

Blood is sometimes used as a symbol in the Bible: Joel 2:31 informs us that the moon will turn to blood before the coming of the Lord. But not too many theologians think the moon will lose its solid mass and turn into liquid of the type found in human arteries. We understand it means that the color of the moon will change to blood red. When Jesus took the cup at the Last Supper he said, "This is my blood," in reality the liquid in the cup was wine, which was symbolic of his blood because of its color.

Science too, may help us with the first plague. Dr. Stephan Pflugmacher, a biologist at the Leibniz Institute for Water Ecology and Inland Fisheries in Berlin, thinks a toxic freshwater algae called Burgundy Blood algae is known to have existed 3,000 years ago and still causes similar effects today. The algae multiplies in slow-moving warm waters with high levels of nutrition, and the water is stained red when the algae dies.

Exodus 7:24 tells us that the Egyptians dug along the Nile because they could not drink the water from the river. That means they were digging down along the banks of the Nile because the water was filtered by the process of sinking through the sandy silted banks similar to how we would run water through a filtering system today. The Nile is the primary fresh water source for Egypt: the river breaks up into its famous delta shape as it reaches Lower Egypt, the Pelusiac branch of the river Nile flowed to the northeast and ran through the fields of Zoan. Further upstream the

3. Ipuwer, "Ancient Egyptian," admonition 2:10.

conditions were providentially favorable for the growth of the cyanobacteria, thus the algae affected the supply of fresh water in the area. The LORD said to Moses, "Tell Aaron, 'Take your staff and stretch out your hand over the waters of Egypt—over the streams and canals, over the ponds and all the reservoirs—and they will turn to blood.' Blood will be everywhere in Egypt, even in vessels of wood and stone" (Exod 7:19). The Egyptians may have previously obtained water in their vessels not realizing the microorganisms were in the water and when the organisms died they dyed the water red.

Pharaoh called for his magicians, who took some water they had previously collected as part of the royal touring party's supply of water, said a few words of incantation over it, and told Pharaoh to wait a while and watch what happens, and sure enough the water turned red. The magicians had probably either seen the phenomenon before, or heard about it from their secret fraternal, which kept a tight rein on their magic-circle of information. Pharaoh was not hard to convince that his magi too, could turn water to blood.

The fish were dead and the water was getting undrinkable, the current state of affairs as they were, meant Pharaoh left the area and travelled the 13 miles back to Avaris. "Pharaoh turned and went back to his palace" (Exod 7:23 gwt).

Seven days passed. The Lord spoke to Moses telling him to go to Pharaoh. This would mean a short journey south for Moses, travelling the same 13 miles to Avaris. The Israelites were situated in the eastern delta and on the eastern side of the ancient Pelusiac branch of the Nile, which once flowed into a coastal lagoon then known as the Lake of Tanis. The waterways of the delta changed over time because of a silting up process and towns and cities would relocate to be close to the fresh water supply. Thutmose III and Amenhotep II had a large palatial precinct within a 14-acre site at Avaris.[4] With the help of the Israelites, the city was developed into a place for stockpiling grain and other foods. The area was also known as Rameses or Pi-Rameses. A scarab belonging to Amenhotep II and a seal from the time of his reign, 1427 to 1401 BC, help date the site. Amenhotep II would be about 37 to 38 years old at the time Moses was confronting him: he became pharaoh at the age of 18, so he'd had 20 years in power before Moses turned up on his doorstep.

Moses and his brother Aaron made the journey to Avaris; Moses was 80 years old and Aaron 83. How keen Amenhotep II was on being told

4. Roehrig, *Hatshepsut*, 75.

what to do by these older men, we can only surmise. Pharaoh knew Moses and Aaron were able to perform some sort of powerful magic, nothing his own enchanters couldn't replicate, but all the same Moses and Aaron had built up a reputation for themselves and on that basis Pharaoh reluctantly admitted them into his precinct. Moses again informs Pharaoh that Yahweh instructs him to let his people go so that they may worship him. If Pharaoh refused to let the Israelites go, the Egyptians would be plagued by frogs. Pharaoh ignored this request. Aaron stretched out his hand over the waters of Egypt and frogs came from the waters. There were pools, canals, and lagoons, as well as the Nile, so as Aaron made his way around each site the frogs appeared. "Can you do this, too?" Pharaoh probably said to his enchanters. There were a few waterways that Aaron had not yet visited so the magicians of Pharaoh took him to one and performed a similar feat.

Science can also help us with the second plague: the arrival of Burgundy Blood algae may have set in motion the events that led to the appearance of the frogs. Hormones that govern development are able to speed up the amphibians' maturation from tadpoles into frogs in times of stress. The arrival of the toxic algae would have triggered such a transformation and forced the frogs to leave the water where they lived.

Pharaoh's enchanters seemed to convince him that they, too, were able to produce frogs from the water. However, they didn't seem to have any way of returning the slimy creatures to the waters. The frogs were truly plaguing the Egyptians: the royal precinct was situated on the eastern bank of the easternmost branch of the Nile, the Pelusiac, so Pharaoh's precinct would be in the direct line of frog-fire. The mucid cold-blooded vertebrates were not creatures you would want in your bed, and the frogs made their way into the palace and into Pharaoh's bedroom and into his bed. They also made their way into the houses of his officials, who were all close by and probably in the precinct itself as the area was so large. The frogs even made it into the royal ovens and kneading troughs.

When the call came from Pharaoh, Moses and Aaron must have praised God thinking their mission had been a success. So, once again, the two brothers made their way to the palace. Sure enough Pharaoh wanted the brothers to "entreat Yahweh" that he may take away the frogs. The first plague affected the water supply, but Pharaoh may have suffered little because he would have servants who would dig for filtered water, so in that respect he was able to bear the first plague without much personal affliction. But the indiscriminating frogs inflicted themselves upon Pharaoh as much as anyone else. Pharaoh made a promise to Moses to "let the people go." Moses remained humble recognizing the leadership of the man he was talking to and said, "Glory over me: when shall I entreat for you." He allowed Pharaoh to decide the time of the prayer to Yahweh. "Glory over me" was probably an expression used in Egypt when speaking with those in authority, and it meant, "I am willing to follow your lead." The expression lets us know that Moses knew how to intercede with Egyptian royalty since we don't hear of the Israelites using this expression. Moses, owing to his royal upbringing, was well acquainted with Egyptian etiquette.

Pharaoh did not want to wait long for "the entreating," "Tomorrow," Pharaoh was quick to reply. So Moses did what Pharaoh requested and the frogs died by the thousands, and were piled up in stinky heaps. The hot climate and sunshine would not help with the smell.

> But when Pharaoh saw that there was relief, he hardened his heart
> and would not listen to Moses and Aaron. (Exod 8:15)

This is bad! We are told in Psalm 15 that he who keeps an oath even when it hurts, and does not change his mind, may live on the Lord's holy mountain and dwell in his sacred tent. Pharaoh could have no fellowship with the Lord.

In the early days of man in Genesis chapter 1, God had fellowship with them, and spoke and walked with them. But since we have learned sin, the Lord has withdrawn himself, he cannot look on sin or be party to it. Moses was acting as a go-between, and in a way, Pharaoh was representing the world. We see from Exodus 8:15 that Pharaoh hardened his own heart, it is a choice we all face.

Moses went back to see Pharaoh to discuss the details of the Israelites' exit and found Pharaoh reneging on his word. So a plague of gnats followed, Pharaoh wasn't given an option about this plague, it came as a result of breaking his word. Aaron struck the dust of the ground with the staff "unsettling" some dust in the process as a sign: Egypt was about to be "unsettled."

With so many piles of rotting frog corpses (and God making sure that the meteorological conditions were fit for his purpose), gnats or mosquitoes would soon be flourishing. One food source for mosquitoes is decaying matter, it's only the female mosquitoes who feed on blood and then only when they need protein to nourish their eggs. But we can be fairly sure that there were plenty of female mosquitoes looking for some additional protein, to the annoyance of the Egyptian people.

Pharaoh's magicians did their best to replicate this plague but could not. Mosquitoes are too unwieldy to manipulate easily. In the end the magicians gave in and admitted to Pharaoh, "This is the finger of God" (Exod 8:19). It is at this point that events took a marked turn for the worse because Pharaoh allowed his heart to develop a new thick layer of callousness—he now had the knowledge that his wise men had given him and was left without excuse. He was declaring war on Yahweh.

Pharaoh was not reading the signs, not because he couldn't read God's writing but because he was ignoring God's writing. A chain of events was being set in motion; clues were given to Pharaoh from when Moses first appeared before him. A staff was turned into a serpent because there was in fact a serpent at work. Rulers in antiquity carried a scepter, which looked like a shepherd's crook or staff—kings were shepherds of their people. Pharaohs carried a scepter signifying their position as head of their people. Moses performed an allegorical drama before Pharaoh's eyes: a staff turned into a snake. Pharaoh's staff was in danger of being turned into a serpent—his rule, his life, his heart were in danger of being lost. God had issued a similar warning to Cain back in the early chapters of Genesis. Jesus said, "What good is it for someone to gain the whole world, yet forfeit their soul?" (Mark 8:36). Pharaoh should have known what the symbolism meant. The Egyptians had a story about a giant serpent called Apep who was the "lord of chaos." He was the opponent of light and peace and the personification of all that was evil. And Apep (or the devil, as we know him) was about to turn Pharaoh into a little image of himself.

The chain of events could have come to an end at any point, but God knew Pharaoh and used him as an example of what a hard heart can do to a human. Proverbs 20:24 (nasb) says, "Man's steps are ordained by the LORD." God sees our hearts and directs our steps accordingly. "I the LORD search the heart and examine the mind, to reward each person according to their conduct, according to what their deeds deserve" (Jer 17:10). Paul talks about God hardening Pharaoh's heart in Romans 9:17: "Scripture says to Pharaoh: 'I raised you up for this very purpose, that I might display my power in you and that my name might be proclaimed in all the earth.'" Paul goes on to say, "One of you will say to me: 'Then why does God still blame us? For who is able to resist his will?' But who are you, a human being, to talk back to God?" (Rom 9:19–20). The main issue that Paul addresses is not how God works in the heart of men but that men's first priority when thinking about such matters is "Don't question God!" When we approach the subject with a humble heart we can see that if God sees a smoking flax he will do all in his power to keep it aflame. As Isaiah 42:3 tells us, "A smoldering wick he will not snuff out." God is not willing that anyone should perish but that all should come to repentance (2 Pet 3:9). That includes Pharaoh too.

The second sign shown to Pharaoh in the divine drama performed by Moses and Aaron was water to blood. This should have made Pharaoh sit up and take notice since blood usually only means one thing, and it's not good. Blood flowing like water is a bad sign for sure, and a severe warning. This chain of events that has been set in motion can end in death, "take notice Pharaoh."

Chapter 17

A Pattern Emerges

TO ESCAPE THE SEVERITY of the mosquitoes at Avaris, Pharaoh, it seems, made his way a few miles northwards back to the fields of Zoan, because Moses is again instructed to "Get up early" and confront Pharaoh as he makes his way to the water. Yahweh again, through Moses, tells Pharaoh to "Let my people go." This time the recompense for not complying with Yahweh's mandate will be swarming flies. This will be the fourth plague Pharaoh and the Egyptians will have to endure. And quite amazingly, the area the Israelites live in will be free from the flies. God wanted Pharaoh to see a distinction between the Israelites and the Egyptians. The route Pharaoh travelled from the fields of Zoan to Avaris borders the land of Goshen so Pharaoh would see the distinction quite clearly.

Pharaoh made no reply to Moses.

The rotting bodies of the frogs make a rich source of organic matter that provides bountiful nutrition for fly larvae. The chain of events continued. We know Pharaoh did not like his personal space invaded, or his person touched by frogs. Pharaoh had been treated like a divine luminary since the age of 18 and probably before that, too. People could not easily approach a pharaoh without his approval, and then there would be some symbolic gestures necessary, but the flies ignored all Egyptian protocol and made their way straight into the living quarters of Pharaoh himself. Dense swarms of flies were inflicted on Pharaoh and his close associates and the people of Egypt. There was rot in the land, but the leader cannot see where the epicenter of the corrosion lies.

Pharaoh made no attempt to contact his magicians to see if they were able to come up with a similar feat, in fact, he seems to have given up totally on his wise men. Once again he summoned Moses and Aaron saying, "Go, sacrifice to your God here in the land" (Exod 8:25). Pharaoh was using a clever political tactic, he appears to grant the petition of Moses but adds the words "here in the land." Moses had always stood firm that the Israelites should be allowed to go three days' journey into the wilderness and then worship, no less could be accepted. Moses thought it right to explain to Pharaoh one reason why they could not accept his terms—the Egyptians had beliefs about some animals being sacred, so Moses points out to Pharaoh, there would be trouble if people saw the Israelites sacrificing some animals to Yahweh. Moses was appealing to the magistrate in Pharaoh, Moses knew that civil unrest is not something rulers want.

"Okay then, go ahead," Pharaoh replied. "I will let you go into the wilderness to offer sacrifices to Yahweh your God. But don't go too far away. Now hurry and pray that I may be rid of these flies" (Exod 8:28).

By the next day the flies had disappeared, not one remained, but Pharaoh failed to issue the order to the Egyptian security officials to allow the Israelites access to the wilderness. He hardened his heart once again, probably reinforcing his troops in Goshen just in case the Israelites tried anything.

For a second time Pharaoh defaulted on his promised word. There was war between Pharaoh and Yahweh; the two parties in conflict were opposites, diametrically opposed to each other in nature and objectives. The Lord, we read in Psalm 89:34, will not violate his covenant or alter what his lips have uttered. He keeps his word. Pharaoh, however, violates his word as soon as the moment is expedient. Moses had explained to Pharaoh that seeing animals being sacrificed would not sit well with the Egyptian people, which is why the Israelite people needed to make the three-day journey. Pharaoh agreed, as long as Moses pleaded with Yahweh for the flies to disappear. Moses kept his side of the deal but now Pharaoh revealed the contents of his heart when he failed to keep his word. As a result the sacrifice of Israelite animals would not take place but instead many animals in Egypt would be sacrificed: this would be the fifth plague.

Animals would be affected in droves: horses, donkeys, cattle, sheep, goats, and even the traders' camels that came into the country from elsewhere. We have seen diseases that affect animals in modern times, foot and mouth disease being one of them, but there are a number of others. The

Ipuwer Papyrus says, "All animals, their hearts weep; cattle moan."[1] This fifth plague would hit Egypt's economy: potential traders would not want to bring their caravans into Egypt to buy and sell if it meant they would lose their camels. Pharaoh made a point of checking to see if any of the animals were affected in the region where the Israelites lived. They weren't.

Still Pharaoh remained hardened. So now, perhaps because Pharaoh was failing to see the allegorical nature and portent of the plagues, Moses and Aaron prepared a piece of drama. Aaron, as we know, worked with the casting of metal, so God told the two brothers to take some handfuls of soot from the furnace. They tossed the soot into the air while Pharaoh was watching and the soot was borne on the wind. No words needed, just a display of silent drama. This is similar to when Aaron struck the dust of the ground and gnats or mosquitoes took their toll on the people. Some versions of the Bible say the dust became gnats, but the Septuagint informs us that Aaron struck the dust of the ground and then the gnats appeared, not that the dust turned into gnats. The symbolic element is that as dust is everywhere so there would be gnats everywhere. A similar scenario took place with the soot. Festering boils broke out and it seems the magicians were hit particularly hard with this plague. They are singled out for a special mention: they "could not stand before Moses because the boils were on them" (Exod 9:11). The population was also afflicted. There are a number of factors that could cause the human population to fall ill. The modern medical diagnosis could be anthrax, where nasty skin lesions can be one of the symptoms. There were certainly enough flies, gnats, and decaying animal corpses to foster a number of diseases that would infect humans, culminating in the sixth plague.

But still, even though the boils hit Pharaoh's skin hard, his heart remained resolute. Consequently, Moses rises early once again and delivers God's frank admission of what he is doing.

> By now I could have stretched out my hand and struck you and your people with a plague that would have wiped you off the earth. But I have raised you up for this very purpose, that I might show you my power and that my name might be proclaimed in all the earth. (Exod 9:15–16)

According to the book of Exodus the reason Pharaoh was in power was to facilitate the proclamation to the world of who God is and what he is

---

1. Ipuwer, "Ancient Egyptian," admonition 5:5.

capable of. God knew what type of person Pharaoh was, he was well aware that Pharaoh would not relent before another king, even before the King of kings, so this particular pharaoh was used as an example that teaches all of us not to oppose God. People still talk about the plagues of Egypt; we are considering them now, all these years later.

This God, Yahweh, was not only God of the Israelites but also of heaven and earth. To display that fact, the seventh plague will come from the skies. Fearsome hail will fall like bullets from the heavens. We then read, "Those officials of Pharaoh who feared the word of the Lord hurried to bring their slaves and their livestock inside. But those who ignored the word of the Lord left their slaves and livestock in the field" (Exod 9:20). We can plainly see that there were people in Egypt who feared the Lord. In the New Testament Peter tells us that "in every nation he that feareth him, and worketh righteousness, is accepted with him" (Acts 10:35 kjv).

But there were some who did not listen and Pharaoh was among them. Moses stretched out his staff towards the sky and a dreadful lightning storm began. The stormy blast thrashed the land of Egypt. Goshen, where the Israelites were situated, remained untouched by the hail. Egyptian crops were spoiled. Ipuwer remarked that "Everywhere barley has perished . . . Indeed, that has perished which yesterday was seen."[2]

Exodus chapter 9 relates an interesting detailed parenthetical sentence towards the end of the chapter that, "(The flax and barley were destroyed, since the barley had headed and the flax was in bloom. The wheat and spelt, however, were not destroyed, because they ripen later)" (Exod 9:31). Ipuwer remarked that, "The land is left over to its weakness like the cutting of flax."[3]

If plagues can be thought of as impressive, the seventh plague falls into that category, and we even see a rare moment of (what looks like) contrition from Pharaoh when he calls for Moses and Aaron confessing that he and his people have sinned. We may need to remember that when Pharaoh said this, the storm was unabated, and he wanted its end. Moses replied,

> When I have gone out of the city, I will spread out my hands in prayer to the Lord. The thunder will stop and there will be no more hail, so you may know that the earth is the Lord's. (Exod 9:29)

This was the lesson that God was teaching, not so much to Pharaoh as to us all. Another king had learned this lesson when he wrote, "The earth is the

2. Ibid., 6:3 and 5:12.
3. Ibid., 5:12.

LORD's, and everything in it" (Ps 24:1). Moses's parting remark to Pharaoh was "I know that you and your officials still do not fear the LORD God" (Exod 9:30). The thunder and lightning was replaced with calm, but Pharaoh's will, remained unchanged.

The eighth plague began when the LORD said to Moses, "Go to Pharaoh, for I have hardened his heart and the hearts of his officials" (Exod 10:1). Another way of looking at the hardening of Pharaoh's heart might be similar to when someone is upset by something that's been said to them. Let's suppose that Dave has made a remark about his friend Mike's work. Mike doesn't take kindly to the remark and so when Dave mentions this to his wife later that evening he may say, "I have made Mike mad, he's not very happy with me at the moment." In a similar way we can think of Yahweh explaining to Moses that he has made Pharaoh angry. He has ruined Pharaoh's crops and caused devastation throughout the land of Egypt and Pharaoh has not taken kindly to any of Yahweh's methods. But Yahweh used the hardness of Pharaoh and his officials' hearts as a lesson, and the world has learned something important from what happened at that point in human history.

At the next juncture locusts appear. There has already been substantial damage to crops, and we remember from the plague of hail that the wheat was not yet ripe. This eighth plague seems to have arrived hot on the heels of the hail and we know that locusts generally eat the grain from heads of wheat while they are still green, so the wheat was ready for the hungry swarming locusts. The Egyptian people would be quick to salvage what they could, and store the remaining crops so that they were hidden away from the locusts. Locust feces, rich in bacterial and fungal organisms, may have contaminated the grain that was still damp from the hail, all of which would have significant implications for the tenth and final plague.

By the time we reach the ninth plague we begin to see a pattern emerging: two plagues with a choice attached to them, then a third with no option. The ninth plague, like the third and sixth, was sent without any previous warning. The Ipuwer Papyrus informs us that, "The land is not light."[4]

Darkness across the land could have been caused by a number of natural means, but some theologians are reluctant to come up with natural causes for all of the plagues. After all it was the magicians of Pharaoh who had earlier confessed that, "This is the finger of God." And let's remember that sometimes people in the Bible whom we don't expect it from speak the truth. The Roman soldier at the crucifixion who made the good confession

4. Gardiner, *Admonitions*, 70.

saying, "Truly this was the Son of God!" (Matt 27:54 nasb). Or Pilate who had a notice prepared and fastened to the cross that read: "Jesus of Nazareth, the king of the Jews" (John 19:19).

The punitive effect of three days of darkness was too much for Pharaoh, and he yields to a greater degree than he ever previously succumbed. Pharaoh had yet to learn that God requires 100 percent obedience from us. We cannot outwit God, or hold his arm behind his back. Pharaoh told Moses that the Israelites could leave but they must leave their livestock behind. Moses finds this compromise unacceptable and explains to Pharaoh his reasons: the livestock will be needed for sacrifices and he is not yet sure which animals each family will have to sacrifice. The exasperated Pharaoh rudely and discourteously tells Moses to "Get thee from me" (Exod 10:28 kjv). Furthermore Pharaoh announced an end to the negotiations, with the proclamation that if Moses saw Pharaoh's face one more time he would surely be put to death.

Pharaoh, not realizing the enormity of what he had said, brings a "death sentence" into the proceedings. He was the first to mention death as a weapon. If we view the engagement between Pharaoh and God as an old-time duel between two persons, we'll remember that a duel usually begins with a choice of weapons, and it seems that in this instance Pharaoh had chosen, and so it would be.

The Lord had already forewarned Moses what the outcome of this final meeting would be, so Moses agreed to the final edict laid down by Pharaoh that Moses would not appear before him again. Moses had previously been told by the Lord that the whole long procedure of asking Pharaoh to be allowed to go three days' journey into the wilderness would now pay off because Pharaoh would soon want to be rid of the Israelites completely, which was, of course, the main objective.

By this time Moses was a bit of a superstar: the Egyptian people, and even the magicians, were in awe of him. No one had taken on Pharaoh like this before. Who was this man and his pastoralist people? While Moses's celebrity status lasted, the Lord told him that the Israelites ought to make good use of his fame and ask their Egyptian neighbors for articles of silver and gold, which the Egyptians willingly gave. The people seemed to realize that something supernatural was afoot in their land and if offerings of gold and silver may be given to those who wielded this power, then so be it.

Ipuwer records that, "Gold and lapis lazuli, silver and turquoise, carnelian and amethyst . . . are strung on the necks of maidservants."[5]

However, the kingpin for the Egyptian people in the painful trial that was about to follow was not the Israelite people, but their own Pharaoh, to whom they all paid allegiance. He had the power to avoid the last and agonizing plague, but chose to ignore Moses's proclamations. So the firstborn sons among the Egyptians, including Pharaoh's own son, would die.

In one way we can see a parallel here. Pharaoh had defied the God of heaven, and placed himself as supreme. He was, after all, thought of as a god among his people, and perhaps he was starting to believe his own publicity. In the New Testament the mother of James and John made a request of Jesus: "Grant that my two sons may sit at your right and left in your kingdom." Jesus told her that she did not know what she was asking. He turned to the two sons and said, "Can you drink the cup I am going to drink?" "We can," they answered (Matt 20:20–22). In a similar way Pharaoh set himself up in God's place, not knowing that God himself would have a sacrifice to make with his own firstborn Son. Pharaoh did not seem to know what he was taking on.

5. Ipuwer, "Ancient Egyptian," admonition 3:2.

Chapter 18

Shaken to the Core

MOSES, "HOT WITH ANGER," left Pharaoh's presence for the last time. The manner of speech used by Moses in this last interchange with Pharaoh had been calm and dignified, but we get a little insight here into how Moses felt since he records his feelings for us. The great lesson of humility which God had taken some pains to teach Moses throughout his life was teetering on the edge and the hot natural temper of his youth ignited but he was able to contain the flames enough to stop them spilling over into his speech. Pharaoh had threatened his life—he had been ignominiously dismissed— he had lost any further rights to an audience with the king, so it's not surprising that Moses was angry. The Septuagint's rendering of Psalm 4:4 says, "Be angry, and do not sin," and the Scripture is quoted in Ephesians 4:26 saying, "In your anger do not sin." Moses gives us a good example of the application of that Scripture.

The tenth and final plague was grave, severe, and heartbreaking. There are theories about possible natural causes for the death of the firstborn, which could have some merit. If lethal mycotoxins had grown on the top layers of the salvaged grain—which had been sodden from the hail and contaminated by the locusts—and the Egyptians allowed the firstborn of the family to eat first, and also served them a larger portion, either through custom or a ceremonial meal, then the firstborn would be most affected by the fungal growth. The Passover occurred on the first full moon following the vernal equinox, so suggesting that the Egyptians had some sort of celebration during that month, particularly at the full moon, may be a suggestion within the realms of possibilities. The Israelites were instructed to eat a different meal that same evening, so the Israelites did not take part in any local custom.

Moses had been told by the Lord to take a good quality lamb, and for each family to eat the meat that particular evening. Any bread that the Israelites ate was specifically made without yeast. This particular "no yeast" command was emphasized in no uncertain terms—if anyone did use yeast they were to be cut off from the people.

> For seven days no yeast is to be found in your houses. And anyone, whether foreigner or native-born, who eats anything with yeast in it must be cut off from the community of Israel. Eat nothing made with yeast. Wherever you live. (Exod 12:19)

So, including the day the Israelites ate the lamb, and for the six days afterwards they could eat no yeast.

We know that fungal spores can grow and multiply fast when the conditions of temperature and humidity are favorable to their growth. Consequently, mycotoxins can be produced which are capable of producing death in humans and animals. Mycotoxins have been implicated in the modern world as agents of chemical warfare.[1] If the tenth plague was caused by a pathogen related to fungal growth, we can see how God protected the Israelites while the Egyptians were left with no advice about eating contaminated grains.

We may prefer to think that God moved through the land of Egypt picking out all those who should die, and that is a point of view, but we would do well to remember that God often uses natural means to bring about his plan. Exodus 15:26 informed the Israelites that if they paid attention to his commands and kept all his decrees, then he would not bring on the Israelite community any of the diseases that the Egyptians suffered from, for Yahweh is the healer. It is God who brings health to humans, and he may use supernatural means occasionally to emphasize a point, such as when Jesus healed the man who was blind and said, "I have come into this world, so that the blind will see and those who see will become blind" (John 9:39). Jesus was talking about a deeper issue but used the miracle of the blind man's eyes being opened to make the point. But often God uses the world he placed around us as the construct in which obedience to his laws works well.

---

1. Bennett and Klich, "Mycotoxins," lines 1–3.

A long time before the invention of the microscope, laws of sanitation were issued to the Israelites. They probably wondered why all these laws were necessary, and interestingly, God showed no interest in teaching them about microorganisms, he simply told them to be obedient and consequently if they followed his laws they would escape the diseases that afflicted the Egyptians. The Lord doesn't always explain the inner workings of scientific processes: he leaves that for humans to find out. Man gave names to the animals, and some of those animals, the very small ones, are still being discovered and named. The Bible is not a scientific textbook, it has a deeper reach than that: God gets on with what is important for a man's immaterial heart, leaving scientists to discover the mechanisms of the material universe.

God issued the laws of sanitation soon after the Israelites had escaped from Egypt. People who touched a dead or diseased animal or person—or even touched bed linen, clothes, or secretions from a sick person—were informed they needed to bathe and wash their clothes. They also needed to avoid contact with others. These instructions sound like modern health and safety rules. Houses that had mold growing were to be scraped and re-plastered or destroyed, to prevent the spread of disease. Porous vessels that came into contact with dead animals were to be broken, since they would harbor bacteria. People showing signs of sickness were to be quarantined, until examined and certified healthy. People were to wash after intercourse. Tattoos and cuttings on the flesh were also forbidden. The probability of contracting an infectious disease was cut right down. Human waste was to be buried well away from human dwellings. These days we know that epidemics of typhus, cholera, and dysentery can be attributed to the waste disposal of sewage into water supplies or nearby streets.

The ancient Egyptian's did have a little idea of how medicine worked and some of their remedies were not totally without value, though some of the treatments would not have a great deal of curative elements to them. We still have some papyruses that record Egyptian prescriptions for ailments. Prescriptions for various complaints could include dung of dog, donkey, and gazelle. Others might be dead mice, moldy bread, lizard blood, putrid meat, stinking fat, and moisture from pigs' ears, to name a few. So it's all the more remarkable that Moses, who had been educated by the Egyptians, suddenly introduced the Israelites to washing, quarantine, and general sanitation. In the Middles Ages when leprosy was a massive problem, physicians at the time said the disease was caused by practices like eating garlic or the meat of diseased hogs or a malign conjunction of the planets. A similar scenario took place for the Black Death that killed 60 million people in the 14th century, when the physicians were seen to be powerless to combat these diseases. The Church at the time (which had a lot more power than it does today), decided to follow the laws laid down for leprosy and sickness introduced by Moses. Once the condition had been diagnosed the patient was segregated from the community, and this proved to be the winning formula against the disease that was killing so many.

Exodus tells us that even animals didn't escape the tenth plague. Moses had previously explained to Pharaoh that the Egyptians would not be happy with the sacrifices the Israelites were about to make, which informs us of the high regard the Egyptian people had for some animals. Exodus 12:12 tells us that God will execute judgement of the gods of Egypt. Animals were used by the Egyptians to signify their gods: cows, bulls, and rams were sacred animals. If firstborn animals were kept for reasons of temple worship then their feed could also be contaminated, so they would also fall foul to the fungi that caused mycoses.

The Passover was a devastating night for the Egyptians. Ipuwer remarks of a time when "He who places his brother in the ground is everywhere."[2] Exodus says "there was loud wailing in Egypt, for there was not a house without someone dead" (Exod 12:30). Amenhotep II, as we have noted, was not a firstborn son so he was untouched; however, he is said to have fathered 10 sons. The son who actually succeeded Amenhotep II on the throne was named Thutmose IV. There are reasons to suppose that Thutmose IV was not the firstborn son of Amenhotep II. Firstly, it seems slightly out of character for Amenhotep II to name his firstborn son after his own father rather than after himself. Secondly, papyrus number 10056 in the British Museum speaks of a Prince Amenhotep. The year dating the manuscript is lost but the month and day correspond to the date of Amenhotep II's accession to the throne, implying that Prince Amenhotep was his son. Thirdly, the Dream Stele of Thutmose IV was erected in the first year of Thutmose IV's reign, 1401 BC. The commemorative stone slab, known as the Dream Stele, was set up between the front paws of the great Sphinx at Giza. The evidence on the stele suggests Thutmose IV was the younger brother whose elder brother—the heir to the throne—died before he could inherit the throne.

2. Ipuwer, "Ancient Egyptian," admonition 2:13.

The Israelites had been told to take some of the blood from the slaughtered lamb and smear some of the blood on the top and sides of the doorframe. If we picture this scenario for a moment, the blood smeared on the top of the doorframe would probably be pulled by gravity downwards, and a few drops may end up on the floor, so with the blood on both sides of the doorframe and also at the top and bottom, the shape of a cross would be formed. Furthermore, the doorframes were probably made of wood, so we get a picture of the cross on which Christ died. The Passover is steeped in lessons. The "no yeast" rule may have had a practical application but it was also a good symbol of sin in our lives. God drew a sharp distinction between Israel and the Egyptians.

> There will be loud wailing throughout Egypt—worse than there has ever been or ever will be again. But among the Israelites not a dog will bark at any person or animal. Then you will know that the Lord makes a distinction between Egypt and Israel. (Exod 11:6–7)

Egypt, including Pharaoh, was shaken to the core. Pharaoh had fought with Yahweh and lost, he was now, at least for the time being, totally broken. The "wailing" in the vicinity of Avaris was heard in the palace, making Pharaoh aware that the impact of the crushing calamity had not fallen on himself alone. He was quick to issue orders that Moses and his people may leave Egypt. The Egyptian people themselves, including Pharaoh's officials and his magicians, were also desperate for the Israelites to be gone.

> The Egyptians urged the people to hurry and leave the country. "For otherwise," they said, "we will all die!" So the people took their dough before the yeast was added, and carried it on their shoulders in kneading troughs wrapped in clothing. The Israelites did as Moses instructed and asked the Egyptians for articles of silver and gold and for clothing. The Lord made the Egyptians favorably disposed toward the people, and they gave them what they asked for; so they plundered the Egyptians. (Exod 12:33–36)

Pharaoh uttered one last phrase in his message to Moses and Aaron—"And also bless me."

Chapter 19

Yahweh's Military Maneuvering

THE EXACT AMOUNT OF time that had passed was 430 years since Abraham left the city of Ur to when the Israelites left the land of Egypt. Abraham headed to Canaan from one end of the Fertile Crescent, and the Israelites left for Canaan from the other end, with 430 years between the two departures. The text of Exodus remarks that it was the "very same day" (Exod 12:41), which tells us that Abraham marked that day as special and told his descendants about it too. The date the Israelites left Egypt was 14th Abib 1406 BC, which means that Abraham first received the promise from Yahweh on 14th Abib 1836 BC. (The month of Abib corresponds roughly to March/April, depending on the course of the moon. Moses and the Israelites called the month Abib. Its name was changed to Nisan after the time of Ezra.) The Masoretic text only mentions time spent in Egypt for the 430 years but the older Septuagint text helps us understand that the 430 years includes all of the sojourning. Paul in the New Testament also uses the Septuagint to quote 430 years from Abraham receiving the promise to when the Law was given, and the Law was given shortly after the exodus (Gal 3:16–18).

We have already worked out that the vast number of people involved in the exodus in our modern Bibles is most likely incorrect, there were probably about 20,000 to perhaps 30,000 people who left Egypt—600 clans or troops of men rather than 600,000. Thirty thousand is still a large number of people, but no more than would gather for a football game in a local town. I have walked along with people at the end of a football game and it's not too difficult as long as people are courteous and watch where they are going.

The Israelites had been located somewhere between Avaris (Rameses) and Zoan on the eastern side of the easternmost branch of the Nile delta. They would need to head to the Wadi Tumilat and the fastest way was a route southeast, which would be a 20-mile journey to Pithom. They could then turn east along the Wadi, which was the way they first came into Egypt. Exodus 12:37 notes for us, that the first port of call for the Israelites was a place called Succoth. You may remember that Jacob, on his way back from northern Mesopotamia, built some temporary shelters before he crossed the river Jordan, and he called the place Succoth, meaning shelters. We find a similar name in Egypt along the Wadi Tumilat. The Israelites had previously helped to build an army store city along the Wadi called Pithom, which was located around the halfway point of the Wadi. When the Israelites were working on the city of Pithom they would have needed temporary shelters as homes while the job was being completed. Perhaps it was those temporary shelters that they called Succoth. So the first leg of the exodus would have been completed in a day, with the people camping at Pithom's temporary shelters. The Lord travelled with the people in a pillar of cloud by day and a pillar of fire by night. He stayed in front of the people leading the way. The next leg of the journey was along the rest of the Wadi to the edge of the desert, a trip of 8 or 9 miles. The place was called Etham and found next to Lake Timsah where the modern-day city of Ismailia is based. The Israelites were located on the edge of freedom, all they had to do was to follow the "way to Shur," the road their forefathers had taken, all the way back to Canaan. But Pharaoh suddenly said, "What have we done? We have let the Israelites go and have lost their services!" So he took six hundred of the best chariots, along with all his other chariots of Egypt accompanied by his officers and set off in pursuit of the Israelites" (Exod 14:5–7).

What happened next was a brilliant piece of strategic military maneuvering on Yahweh's part. To get a clear picture we need to remember that there were two basic roads into the Egyptian delta from the east. "The way of the sea" is one, and was sometimes called "the way of the Philistines," the Romans later called it "Via Maris," and the Egyptians called it the "Horus way." It was the coastal road from Canaan into Egypt and it can be clearly seen today as the main road that hugs the Mediterranean coast from Israel to Egypt. The other road entered Egypt about 25 miles further south and was called "the way to Shur." This road makes its way through Canaan and culminates in the Wadi Tumilat, where it was joined by the King's Highway for the last part of its journey. Further east the way to Shur passed the Canaanite town of Beersheba, which led nicely onto the Judean ridge route that Abraham had travelled so often. When the Old Testament mentions the "Wadi of Egypt," such as in Isaiah 27:12, "from the flowing Euphrates to the Wadi of Egypt," the Wadi Tumilat is what the text is probably referring to.

When the Israelites first began their exodus, we are told:

> When Pharaoh let the people go, God did not lead them on the road through the Philistine country, though that was shorter. For God said, "If they face war, they might change their minds and return to Egypt." So God led the people around by the desert road. (Exod 13:17–18)

Instead of taking the "way of the Philistines" or the "Horus way," as the Egyptians called it, they headed to the Wadi Tumilat in a southeast direction.

The "Horus way" was garrisoned with a number of Egyptian forts and towers, and the fortifications are described on the walls of the Karnak Temple in Luxor. Archaeological work on the Horus way is ongoing and one fort with several towers has recently been found near the Suez Canal, close to where the Horus way was located. The Horus way needed military watchtowers and forts because the route was open to a number of northern people groups who could use it to attack Egypt. The Hyksos had previously been a worry for the Egyptians and there were other groups of people whom Egypt had to keep an eye out for. So when we read that the Israelites might face war along the Horus way, it could easily have been the Egyptian troops who were stationed there that Israel would be at war with. Pharaoh only had to change his mind and those troops would quickly receive orders to attack the Israelites and turn them around back to Egypt. Yahweh knew this, and also knew that Pharaoh would indeed change his mind. So the Israelites' journey southeast to the Wadi Tumilat was the preferred route. However, once they reached the end of the Wadi, Yahweh told them to "turn back" and "camp between Migdol and the sea." The word "Migdol" means tower, and Ezekiel tells us that Migdol is in the north of Egypt, and he prophesies that the land of Egypt will be laid waste from Migdol to Aswan (Ezek 29:10). In other words, laid waste from the north to the south of Egypt. Migdol was a fortification on the Horus way, but the Israelites were told to stop short of Migdol, they had specific instructions to place themselves between Migdol and the sea. This does not mean the Mediterranean Sea, which is referred to as the "great sea," this sea was the "Sea of Reeds."

Three place names were given to Moses to locate the Israelites in exactly the correct position for God to blow the Sea of Reeds in two. The first was Migdol and the second was Pi Hahiroth, which is a mixture of an Egyptian word Pi ("house" or "the area of," such as in the city of Pi-Rameses), and a Semitic word Hahiroth, which means to "carve" or "cut into." Archaeologists have found a large ancient canal in the area that was cut 500 years prior to the time of Moses. It was used by successive generations though would have been in disuse by the time of Moses, but Pi Hahiroth may well have been a landmark and a well known place name for people who lived in Lower Egypt. The third place name is Baal Zephon, which means "Baal of the north," a god adopted by the Egyptians, placed, superstitiously, on their exposed northeastern frontier.

As a tactical move Yahweh instructed the Israelites to head back towards the Horus way. Pharaoh would be aware of the movements of the group of Israelites, and when he saw that they decided not to endure the hardships of the way of Shur, which headed through the wilderness, he decided to make his move. Yahweh, the chess player, had made his move and knew that Pharaoh would not resist this opportunity to recapture the Israelites. Pharaoh had said,

> What have we done? We have let the Israelites go and have lost
> their services! (Exod 14:5)

So Yahweh, without touching Pharaoh's inner being and free will, had been able to harden the pharaoh's heart once more.

Three days would have passed since the people left the area of Goshen. The Israelites left by divisions, this was no ramshackle group of people ambling down the road, they marched like an army—600 clans, troops, or families. "Thus the Israelites left Egypt like an army ready for battle" (Exod 13:18 nlt). Early on the third day they would need to set out from their camp at Etham, positioned at the end of the Wadi Tumilat, and take the desert track back up north towards the Horus way. The 24 or so miles this journey took was a longer journey than they had travelled so far but the people could see some sort of pillar of cloud in front of them, which Moses had told them was Yahweh's presence, so they were fortified with strength and courage for the march, knowing that God was marching with them. Twenty-four miles is a good distance for a group of people to manage and some of the trek would probably be made as evening encroached upon them. However, as dusk began to fall the pillar of cloud radiated a glow of light that shone on the travellers enabling them to see where their footsteps landed. Their caravan had headlights, and the people made it safely to their destination between Migdol to the north and the Sea of Reeds to the east.

If the people had gone all the way to Migdol they could have turned east and walked across the Horus way land bridge, but by this time the Egyptian army had taken up a strong position cutting off the route to the Horus way. In antiquity there were several freshwater lakes that ran along the edge of the wilderness, roughly corresponding to where the Suez Canal runs in our modern world. The flooding of the Nile was a regular event in those days that would bring fresh water to the flat landscape and help in making some of the ground arable. These days we have the Aswan Dam in Upper Egypt so flooding is not an issue, but in ancient Egypt canals or natural wadis were used as flood safety valves. The end of the Wadi Tumilat had a lake called Timsah, which is still there today and has been incorporated as part of the Suez Canal. Further north was Ballah Lake, which has lost most of its water since the construction of the Suez Canal that drained the lake's waters. To the south of Lake Timsah are the Bitter Lakes, the series of lakes that lie in a natural tectonic rift and fill up with floodwaters from the Nile. If the floodwaters are particularly strong, then salt water from the Gulf of Suez may mingle with the lakes.

On a map, the Gulf of Suez rift can be clearly seen looking at the Red Sea, which has a western and eastern branch at its northern end. The eastern branch is the Gulf of Aqaba, created by a fault line that runs northwards through the Dead Sea in Israel, and the western branch of the Red Sea is called the Gulf of Suez, which is a rift that runs to the Mediterranean Sea. The natural depression of the rift lends itself to Nile floodwaters gathering there. The Suez Canal has now joined the Gulf of Suez to the Mediterranean Sea, which is very helpful for shipping and freight logistics. Ships from the west are no longer forced to travel around the African coastline to get to India and other countries; they can simply sail into the Mediterranean Sea and maneuver along the Suez Canal into the Red Sea and then on to their destination. The shortcut saves some 4,900 nautical miles.

In between the westerly Gulf of Suez and the eastern Gulf of Aqaba lies the triangular shaped Sinai Peninsula. Looking at the Gulf of Suez on a topographical map, we are able to see that the rift in which the freshwater lakes lie is flat land that sits roughly at sea level. In ancient times the landscape and lakes moved position because the Nile itself moved position. The river Nile is over 4,000 miles long, ending in the Nile delta where it breaks up into different branches that empty into the Mediterranean Sea.

The branches of the delta have often changed over time because the long river brings much slit with it and the river's branches in the delta get silted up and stop flowing, leaving a branch to change course and find another route. Sometimes whole cities have had to "up and move" because their water supply has changed course.

The Hebrew word for the body of water the Israelites crossed when leaving Egypt is called *yam suph*, "Sea of Reeds," not Red Sea, though *yam suph* has been rendered "Red Sea" in most modern translations. The Red Sea phrase first came into use with the Septuagint; its translators made *yam suph* ("Sea of Reeds") into *eruthrá thálassē* ("Red Sea"). The Latin Vulgate followed their lead with *mari Rubro* ("Red Sea") and most English versions continued that tradition. Red Sea was not a translation at all, but we ought not to think of their rendering as a mistake: the translators of the Septuagint were intelligent people and changing "Sea of Reeds" to "Red Sea" must have had some basis in their geographical understanding of the region at that time. The Israelites crossed a significant body of water on Egypt's eastern border, and the Septuagint translators connected it with the body of water they knew as the Red Sea when they translated the Septuagint some 1,100 years after the actual crossing. Perhaps the lakes that lay in the Gulf of Suez rift were mingled with the waters of the Red Sea at the time the Septuagint was translated and people of their day knew the waters as an extension of the Red Sea. When Moses first wrote down his experiences he called the waters Sea of Reeds, named because reeds would grow in the freshwater lakes. Not too long after the Israelites had left Egypt, the first attempts began at cutting a canal to link the Red Sea (the Gulf of Suez) with the northeast Egyptian delta coastline. Necho II, who was king of Egypt in 610 BC, made the most serious attempt, but the effort of digging the canal is reputed to have cost 100,000 lives. And after some neglect, Persia's King Darius rebuilt the canal in 522 BC. The canal is said to have been extended to the Red Sea by Polemy II in 285 BC, which is the same timeframe the Septuagint was being translated, so the lakes could have been mingled with Red Sea waters at that point in time, which may be why the translators chose the Red Sea as a name.

Over time the Romans did not maintain the canal and it fell into disrepair and silted up. Various attempts have been tried or thought about since then, even Napoleon Bonaparte had plans drawn up but was let down by a miscalculation at the planning stage. The modern Suez Canal was opened in 1869 and has been a useful line of passage for shipping in the modern world.

Chapter 20

The Parting

FOOD IS AN IMPORTANT issue and 20,000 people or more need feeding, especially if they are on the march. We know they had a supply of bread:

> The people took their dough before the yeast was added, and carried it on their shoulders in kneading troughs wrapped in cloth. (Exod 12:34)

We also read:

> With the dough the Israelites had brought from Egypt, they baked loaves of unleavened bread. The dough was without yeast because they had been driven out of Egypt and did not have time to prepare food for themselves. (Exod 12:39)

We know the Israelites were told not to add yeast to bread, and not to leave any of the cooked lamb until morning. There seems to have been some airborne spores around that were growing on bread or dead animals. The Israelites needed to obey every instruction they had received from Yahweh, then "he will not permit the destroyer to enter your houses and strike you down (Exod 12:23). The verse at Exodus 12:39 seems to say that the reason the bread was unleavened (without yeast added) was because they left in a hurry and didn't have time to add it. But that is not the case, because they were instructed not to add yeast. A quick look at the Hebrew words tells us that they didn't have time to "bake the bread" so they baked the unleavened bread after they had moved out.

The first camp was at Succoth, where they had their first opportunity to bake some of the dough that would give them complex carbohydrates, useful for a steady release of energy as they marched. The second night at Etham they would also eat from the same batch of bread, plus, if needed, they could slaughter some of the animals they had with them. Etham is close to Lake Timsah, so a good supply of fresh water was there for the people and animals to drink. Because of the short journey from Succoth to Etham the people would have a chance to refresh themselves. On the third day an early start was required. They would head northward following the west coast of the freshwater lakes; hence, they had no problem giving thirsty people on the march plenty of water. The lake, which was called Ballah, spread itself up to the land bridge at the Horus way. Once the people reached their appointed destination just short of Migdol, which was situated on the Horus way, they had a short space of time to rest and eat the remainder of the bread.

Pharaoh's compound at Avaris was situated on the eastern bank of the easternmost branch of the Nile, the Pelusiac branch, which emptied into the Mediterranean Sea at the city of Pelusium. Pharaoh would not need to cross this river as he headed along the Horus way to Migdol, where the road went straight through to the land bridge. The land bridge itself may be obscured when the Nile flooded and water from the Pelusiac branch would overflow and pour into Ballah Lake. The flooding occurred from July to September, the exodus occurred in April so the Horus way was free to be travelled. Pharaoh had supposed that the Israelites couldn't face the arduous "way to Shur" because it led to the wilderness, so he reasoned that the Israelites were making their way up the western side of Ballah Lake to the easier route out of Egypt, the Horus way. He made ready his 600 best chariots, plus other chariots of a lesser quality and marshalled his troops, doing his best to arrive at Migdol before the Israelites, thus cutting off their route of escape.

Pharaoh made good time and arrived at Migdol but saw that the Israelites had not yet arrived. He could see they were further down the west coast of Ballah Lake, in fact, he saw they had made camp. The day was almost spent and it looked as though they were down for the night and would resume their journey the next day. So Pharaoh gave the order to his troops to turn south and head towards the Israelite camp. Both sides could see each other: the distance was not great.

The Egyptian army could see the Israelites, and the Israelites could see the Egyptian army. This standoff caused some serious panic among the Israelites, and in their terror and trepidation they turned on Moses, saying, "Didn't we say to you in Egypt, 'Leave us alone; let us serve the Egyptians?'" (Exod 14:12). Moses told them to "Stand firm." He took the part of a strong leader to the Israelites, exercising his experience of time spent with Thutmose III who was an excellent military leader. But when Moses was on his own and close to the pillar of cloud he cried out to the Lord. The Lord said, "Why are you crying out to me?" This was not a time for crying out, but for action. The Lord expressed surprise that Moses didn't realize he had within his grasp the power to command the wind and waves—"Tell the Israelites to move"—but because of where the Egyptian army stood there was nowhere to move except to walk towards Ballah Lake, what the Hebrew Masoretic text calls the Sea of Reeds. The pillar of cloud that had been leading the way now moved around the group and positioned itself as a barrier between the Egyptian army and the Israelites. Dusk closed in early that night for the Egyptian soldiers, a low lying mist seemed to them to make any further attempts to move in on the Israelites futile, and so they made camp for the night. On the other side of the cloud a brightness was radiating among the Israelites. Moses raised his staff and stretched out his hand over the sea and all that night the Lord drove the water back with a strong east wind.

People sometimes wonder if the dividing of the Sea of Reeds was a miracle or an act of divine providence using natural means. The book of Exodus gives us the answer to that question. The Lord was again going to harden the hearts of the Egyptians. We have seen how God has used natural means to reveal what was in Pharaoh's heart. When Pharaoh saw that a plague had passed and he had had time to reflect that the plague in question was probably a natural phenomenon, then his heart would harden and his oppressive designs on the Israelite people continued. So if God was going to reveal what was in Pharaoh's heart once again, then he needed the dividing of the sea to look like it was a natural event. If Pharaoh thought that Yahweh was performing a miracle for the Israelites to walk through the Sea of Reeds then he would not issue the order for his charioteers to give chase. He and the Egyptian commanders were not dull or unintelligent, they would know that an ambush would be the likely result if they pursued the Israelites through the dry seabed.

But what about the wall of water that stood to the left and right that we read about in Exodus 14:22? A wall of water certainly sounds miraculous.

When protection is mentioned in the Bible it is often called a wall. There are a number of examples, but let us look at one: when a servant of the wicked Nabal told Nabal's wife Abigail that David and his group of men were good to them, he did it by saying, "Night and day they were a wall around us the whole time we were herding our sheep near them" (1 Sam 25:16). The New American Standard Bible and a few other translations say, "the waters *were like* a wall to them on their right hand and on their left" (Exod 14:22).

Exodus is clear that a wind divided the water, and the Egyptian army thought so too, *it's just a strong wind that happens from time to time,* and so they were happy to pursue the Israelites into the dry Ballah Lake region.

Work and experimentation has been conducted to show how a strong steady persistent wind, known as a "wind setdown," can move a body of water. Testimonies of people who have seen such a wind setdown's effect upon a body of water have also been recorded. In Moses's case, a sandbar that lent itself to the geological requirements of a pathway for a large group of people appeared during the night. That is why the Israelites were given such specific directions of the location they needed to arrive at on this leg of their journey, we might say that the coordinates were given to them with military precision. Before dawn had fully broken, the Israelite travellers could clearly see a pathway through the water and made haste to use it as a route of escape from the Egyptian army. As the last few escapees were making their way across the bed of the lake, the mist obscuring the army's view lifted and with the aid of an eerie light the Egyptians could just about see the last few Israelites hurrying to get to the other side.

The water of the lakes on the Egyptian delta's eastern border would change shape and depth depending on the time of year. The Egyptians did not seem to think it odd that a ridge had appeared. Some sort of fog had obscured their view but when the haze cleared they lost no time in pursuing their erstwhile workforce. The charioteer corps moved along the newly opened corridor hoping to do what their chariots were suited for—the pursuit of a fleeing enemy on an open plain, where spears could be thrown to inflict casualties on the victims who were fleeing. The Israelites knew this, and it was the threat of arrows and spears that the Egyptians hoped to use as intimidation to make the Israelites give up their journey and surrender—if only the Egyptian army could get close enough to use that power of intimidation.

Chariots were much more dependent on terrain than foot soldiers. They were most effective on flat, dry plains, without boulders, debris, or wet topsoil impeding their advance or even causing their breakdown. Pharaoh had committed his best chariots to the cause of regaining the services of the Israelites, so he stood to lose a large quantity of his military hardware if this operation went awry. Pharaoh himself did not lead this attack but ordered the offensive from the shoreline. Exodus lets us know that all of Pharaoh's horses and chariots followed the Israelites into the sea, but we are not told that Pharaoh or his foot soldiers did. The unwieldy nature of the chariots on terrain that had recently been covered in water proved to be a serious hindrance, and some of the wheels actually broke away from their chariots. The men who made up the Egyptian army had thoughts at the back of their minds of all the previous plagues that Moses claimed were the work of Yahweh, so when the chariots proved difficult to steer, panic set in among them. Pharaoh was not there to order the men to stay in formation so they broke rank and tried to get out of the channel of dry land between the waters.

Military mayhem must have been the result of no commander, spooked charioteers, and unwieldy chariot wheels. While this was taking place Yahweh told Moses to stretch out his hand over the sea once more, and as the full light of day began to emerge, gravity began to pull the waters back to their natural resting place. The daylight revealed to the Egyptian army their immediate danger: water was speedily advancing on either side, and threatening to fill up the channel. The Egyptians tried in vain to outrun the advancing waters but their chariot wheels clogged. The chariots were also encumbered with armor and horses, so they made labored progress over the soft and slimy ground, and while they were still some way from shore, the floods were upon them, and overwhelmed them.

Pharaoh must have seemed a lonely, shocked, and forlorn figure as he made his way back to Avaris with a small retinue of personal aides and foot soldiers. Pharaoh Amenhotep II held military campaigns in the early part of his tenure but any offensive operations in his administration's later years seem to be absent. Egyptologist Claude Vandersleyen remarks that "this relative military inertness lasted until Horemheb's coming to power."[1] Pharaoh Horemheb came to power over 70 years later—losing so much military hardware in the Sea of Reeds left the Egyptians with a lowered military capability and probably little stomach for fighting for some years to come.

Pharaoh, in a rare moment of humility, had previously asked Moses to intercede for him: "And also bless me" (Exod 12:32). Not many people can expect to fight Yahweh and come away unscathed. Jacob fought Yahweh in

1. Vandersleyen, *L'Égypte*, 333, quoted in Petrovich, "Amenhotep II," fn81.

a wrestling match and overcame, but was left with a limp. Pharaoh and his people had fought God at great cost, but God will honor genuine humility and Pharaoh's request saved his life. We do not read that Pharaoh himself died in the waters that covered his army, we read in Exodus 14:27 and Psalm 136:15 that God overthrew Pharaoh and his army in the Red Sea. In Hebrew "overthrow" does not mean to drown but rather "shake off." The Hebrew wording of Exodus 14:28, "The chariots, and the horsemen, and all the host," needs to be read carefully. The Hebrew runs like this: "The chariots and the horsemen (who were) all the host of Pharaoh that came into the sea," implies that his footmen had not yet entered the sea.

Pharaoh Amenhotep II lived a few more years and died in 1401 BC, 5 years after the exodus. The cause of death is unknown. His mummified remains now reside at Cairo Museum, where a photograph of his body clearly shows raised nodules on his neck, which are reported to be on his body too. An x-ray analysis of his mummy reported him to be around the 40-year-old mark when he died. He had reigned in Egypt for over 20 years. After Amenhotep II's death, his palace at Avaris was abandoned.[2]

2. Roehrig, *Hatshepsut*, 79.

Chapter 21

Lessons in Trust

THE EGYPTIAN CHARIOTS, THEIR drivers and passengers, plus their cavalry had been lost. The Israelites looked back across the Sea of Reeds, which was not too wide, and saw bodies lying on the shoreline. The former slaves were now free and began their new era by putting their trust in Yahweh, because they had seen firsthand what he was capable of.

The previous day had been a long one and the early morning walk through the lakebed was arduous, so now that no one was pursuing them they had a chance to rest and regroup. They knew the presence of the Lord was with them and Moses felt inspired to compose a song. Moses himself is too modest to admit that he wrote it but the ode bears some resemblance to Egyptian poetry that Moses would have been exposed to in his earlier years. The poetry and composition of the song is artistic and masterful. The Israelite community would most probably have a practiced set of melodies that words could be matched to. Moses chose a certain meter and wrote down his words. Later in the day he sang the words to the community who entered into the song. Miriam sang the short refrain:

> Sing to the LORD
>> For he is highly exalted.
> The horse and its rider
>> He has hurled into the sea.

The early Semitic dialect that the Israelites spoke may have had the refrain's last word of line two, "exalted," rhyming or matching in rhythm with the last two words of line four, "the sea." The chant would echo around the community. Yahweh would be praised with passion.

After a day's rest on the eastern side of the Sea of Reeds, Moses moved the Israelite community on in a southward direction to the desert of Shur, also known as Etham. This journey took them south along the eastern side of Ballah Lake. In other words they were making the return journey towards Etham, located at the eastern end of the Wadi Tumilat, but this time they were travelling on the eastern side of the freshwater lakes, so they still had access to fresh water. They would reach Etham and Lake Timsah after about a day and a half of travelling. The pace would be slower now that they were not engaged in any military maneuverings. They had animals with them but perhaps not as many as we would imagine. When Jacob's family first settled in Goshen they were shepherds, and would have some herds. But when the 18th Dynasty took control and saw that the Israelites were prospering, they oppressed them and changed their job description. So the Egyptians may have confiscated the Israelites' animals when the Israelites were forced into various Egyptian building projects. Some animals would have remained because the Egyptians knew their workforce needed to eat, but the large herds the Israelites once had may not have been there in such great numbers at the time of the exodus.

The Israelites were not alone in leaving Egypt. Exodus 12:38 (kjv) states that "a mixed multitude went up also with them; and flocks, and herds, *even* very much cattle." Reading the Hebrew text, the "very much" could refer to the whole group just mentioned (i.e., the mixed multitude of people, the flocks and herds). In other words the Israelites were a big group but there was also a large group of people and animals that were not central to the story.

So who were the people within the "mixed multitude"? We are not told of the component parts of this group. But we do know they were not that helpful as we hear of them "murmuring" in Numbers 11:4. Some may have been Egyptians, impressed by the recent miracles, and some undoubtedly were foreign slaves, like the Israelites, glad to escape from their hard taskmasters.

As the group travelled southwards and past Lake Timsah the freshwater lakes began to disappear. Progress would not be fast at this stage: weary travellers would be looking for the next freshwater lake to appear. The time of the Nile flood was still six weeks or so away, so when they came to the next marshy lake they found it to be at a low level and that meant the salty landscape it lay in affected the water. The text reads, "they could not drink the waters of Marah, for they were bitter; therefore it was named Marah" (Exod 15:23). We still call the lakes of that area the Bitter Lakes. These days we have the Great Bitter Lake and the Small Bitter Lake, and the water is fed into them by the Suez Canal. The same depressions in the landscape would probably have been there as Moses led the people alongside that area. The book of Exodus informs us that they could not drink the "waters," probably meaning more than one lake. In Arabic, bitter is *murra* or *murrah*. The Septuagint spells Marah with two r's as Merrah, closer to modern Arabic's *murrah*.

The people needed to drink but the water was not drinking water, and they began to grumble. Moses took the brunt of the murmuring and reached out to Yahweh, who had been on the journey with them:

> Moses cried out to the LORD, and the LORD showed him a piece of wood. He threw it into the water, and the water became sweet. (Exod 15:25)

The Lord often uses natural events to bring about his means, and as he instructed Moses what to do to make the waters sweet, there could have been heavy rainfall elsewhere so fresh water would pour into the low lying Bitter Lakes. But we also do well to remember that Yahweh was not without power. So whether it was by natural means or supernatural means that the waters of Marah were made drinkable, it was Yahweh who actioned it. He also needed to talk to the Israelites about their grumbling and promised them that if they paid attention to his commands, then none of the diseases that afflicted the Egyptians would be upon them. Avoiding disease was a major advantage for any people group so they needed to "listen up." Grumbling, griping, and groaning were not on the agenda for Yahweh's people. They had seen God heal the bitter waters and turn them sweet, and now his healing would be upon them. No bitterness in their hearts would be allowed, only sweet waters should be flowing through them. They would find that obeying God would pay dividends not only for their spiritual health but also for their biological health. But they needed to stop grumbling against Moses because hygiene was a part of the ceremonial law that Moses would soon administer to them and that law would help to keep them free from bacteria. And without the Israelites even knowing there was such a thing as bacteria, there is a good lesson in trust for us all there.

Once refreshed by the sweet water, the Israelites move further south. They would reach the Gulf of Suez after a 25-mile journey from the Bitter Lakes. Then, hugging the eastern coastline of the Gulf of Suez for 4.5 miles from where the Suez Canal joins the Gulf of Suez, there is a place where palm trees can be seen and a well of water. On modern maps the area is called Ayun Musa, which means "wells of Moses." Exodus calls the area Elim. The Israelites set up camp there by the sea, which was about half a mile away from the palm trees, trees that are still there today. Their stay at the camp lasted over two weeks. Exactly one month after they left their homes in Egypt, the 15th day of the second month, Ziv, they were on the move again.

Chapter 22

Grumbling, Griping, and Grousing

THE TIME SPENT AT Elim must have been like a vacation: there were date palm trees, fresh water, and, of course, the sea. The young children and teenagers must have had a whale of a time. In fact, there is a resort there now where people go for a break. The Israelites would not be too enthusiastic about moving on, but move on they must. A plan was afoot and Moses knew the plan, and Aaron probably had a good idea because he had trod this path before. They were following the road to the mines at Serabit el-Khadim. We know from Numbers chapter 33 that the Lord told Moses to write down every stage along the way as a record so that you and I may read about it, and Numbers chapter 33 neatly lays out each stage of the journey for us to read. The book of Exodus gives us the general picture we need to know about the route. A modern map will show us the route they took. From Elim (Ayun Musa or Uyun Musa) they followed what is now the modern coastal road in a southward direction along the east of the Gulf of Suez. Where the road has a sharp turn left, at Hosan Abu Zenna, they made camp, calling it the desert of Sin. The journey between Elim and the desert of Sin was about 50 miles and was a two-stage journey with a stay by the Gulf of Suez at the 25-mile point.

Any Israelites who had worked in the mines at Serabit el-Khadim must have figured out by now where the group was heading, and all doubts would disappear when a sharp left turn was made taking them to Dophkah, which is probably situated in modern-day Qattar Dafari where a well is to be found. This was the route to the mines and the men in the group who had been there before knew it. They also knew that when a mining expedition took place it was planned well in advance with many provisions taken, and orders that were placed with traders who arranged animals to be brought to the mine for a plentiful supply of food for the workers to eat. Moses was most likely on one such errand when he first encountered the burning bush. But, worryingly for the people involved in the exodus, no such provisions had been made for the Israelites' journey.

When Moses first spoke with Yahweh on Mount Horeb, Moses was told that once the people were brought out of Egypt they would worship God on that same mountain (Exod 3:12). Mount Horeb is where the people were now heading, that would be their destination and they would be located there for just under a year. God wanted to take some time teaching them a few important lessons. They were a new nation and needed guidance, they had not been in charge of their own affairs while they were slaves, but now things were different and a good system of law is necessary for any nation if it is going to thrive.

Some of the men were probably saying, "This is the route to the turquoise and copper mine. There's no way we'll find food there unless it's been previously arranged, and it's my guess that Moses or Aaron, our beloved leaders, have overlooked that little fact."

All this time, a steady column of smoke had been moving some way in front of the company of people. Only Moses and Aaron could get close to the column. God chose to reveal himself in this way to the people. Moses could speak with the Lord and relay messages back to the people but God would not get too close to the people. They had begun to grumble for a second time and despite the wonders they had seen, a surly spirit was among them. God cannot be party to any wrongdoing and so kept his distance.

The people were correct in supposing they were heading for the mines, because that's where Mount Horeb and Mount Sinai are located. Traditionally, Mount Sinai was 60 miles further south in Saint Catherine, at an elevation of 5,085 feet. Josephus thought Mount Sinai was the highest mountain in the area. Other mountains have been suggested as contenders for being Mount Sinai, even as far as Midian, but the people of Israel could only move so far in the timescale allotted. Moses and some of his people knew the route so well that they were able to write down the place names of each stop along the way, revealing to us that they had previously journeyed that way—the men who worked in the mines had travelled this route before, and some of them knew it well.

Furthermore, Exodus 16:1 explains to us that the desert of Sin lies between Elim and Sinai. If we look at a map we find that the desert of Sin (Hosan Abu Zenna) lies at the exact halfway point between Elim (Ayun Musa) and Jabal Sāniyah (near the mining complex at Serabit el-Khadim).

The mountains around Serabit el-Khadim are not too high, and can be climbed by an able-bodied person quite well. Presently, Serabit el-Khadim has a pathway that can be walked up, which is said to be "not a very strenuous walk." Jabal Sāniyah (Mount Sinai) is 3 miles from Serabit el-Khadim, and Jabal Ghorâbi (Mount Horeb) lies the other side of a short sandy stretch from both Jabal Sāniyah and Serabit el-Khadim, and is just over 4 miles from Serabit el-Khadim.

The route the Israelites took is not too difficult for us to follow on a map. The rough tracks, roads, or trails that were used in those days followed the lay of the land that lends itself to a track for people to travel along. In modern times we often use the same methods for constructing roads: we follow the lay of the land that lends itself to negotiate hills and mountains the most effective way for travel. So if we look at a good modern road map of the Sinai Peninsula we can see that when the Israelites turned eastward leaving the 66 coastal road at Abu Zenima which took them through to reach Dophkah (Qattar Dafari), the modern map has a road or trail leading around to Serabit el-Khadim. We are informed by the tourist industry that getting to Serabit el-Khadim is half the fun—from the coastal town of Abu Zenima it is mostly off road, although at times there is a sudden stretch of asphalt road that soon disappears again in the sandy desert—a jeep is recommended for the journey.

The Israelites had no jeeps and the inland terrain that took them through to the mining area needed to be negotiated with care. The journey is less than 20 miles, yet two more stops along the way were necessary. The tourist industry may tell us that half the fun is getting to Serabit el-Khadim but the Israelites and the extra people they had with them may not have viewed it as fun.

> Would to God we had died by the hand of the LORD in the land of Egypt, when we sat by the flesh pots, *and* when we did eat bread to the full; for ye have brought us forth into this wilderness, to kill this whole assembly with hunger. (Exod 16:3 kjv)

That verse gives us a flavor of the discontent aimed towards Moses and Aaron and ultimately to the Lord too. Yes, there would be some hardships along the way, there always are when journeys are made, we can't expect to have all the comforts of home when we are on the road. But the journey would not be long. We know from the book of Numbers that the enslaved people of Egypt had fish, cucumbers, melons, leeks, onions, and garlic. These particular edibles were on the minds of the Israelites and the more they talked about them the more they wanted them. The Lord's plan was for them to endure a little hardship in Sinai while they were given the necessary laws their nation would need to live by in the land they were heading to, but once the laws had been written down they would soon be off towards their promised land. The procedure should have taken well under two years and the people would view the land at their journey's end, where they would see clusters of grapes that needed two men to carry on a pole along with pomegranates and figs, plus much more nutritious fare.

The Lord had already spoken to the people about their grumbling and Moses let the people know that Yahweh had again heard their grumbling. (Paul, in 1 Corinthians 10:10, points us to this period as an example from which we can learn, saying, "do not grumble, as some of them did.") The Lord, in turn, let Moses know that he would be raining down "bread from heaven" for the people to eat. What a picturesque phrase, "bread from heaven," what a scene it conjures up. How nutritious that bread must have been, with elements necessary for biological human life to thrive, with a delicious taste, and the knowledge that it was delivered through supernatural means. In the bread we see a picture of Jesus, who called himself the bread that came down from heaven (John 6:51). Christ also broke the bread and told his disciples to eat it, saying, "This is my body given for you: do this in remembrance of me" (Luke 22:19).

The bread that fell from heaven they labelled *manna*. They were told to collect a measure of it each morning for each person. On the sixth day twice as much was to be collected so that the following day could be a day free from servile labor.

The Egyptians seemed to have no concept of a weekly day of rest, but in contrast, at the other end of the Fertile Crescent, the Mesopotamians did have a particular day, that was marked off in sevens, as a special day. In the creation account we see God instituting a day free from work. The garden of Eden, where Yahweh would have passed on this information to Adam, was based in southern Mesopotamia, so it's little surprise that the people of the area got to hear of the Sabbath rest day. Adam's posterity, through to Abraham, knew the story of the 7th day of rest. The weekly day free from oppressive labor must have been a distant memory for the Israelites who were enslaved by the Egyptians. But now, here in Sinai, God is restoring the weekly day of rest to the Israelites.

God also said he would send the people meat. Quail is a small round bird that regularly migrates from Syria and Arabia in the autumn for the purpose of wintering in Central Africa. The quail is similar to grouse and is from the same order of game birds. During their stay in Africa the quail feed well and get plump. When the African weather proves too hot for the birds they make their way north returning en masse in the spring. Their migration is made in stages and being exhausted after the flight over the Gulf of Suez, the birds drop to the ground as soon as they reach the coast, it is then easy to either catch the birds with the hand or to trap them with a makeshift net. Providentially, the Israelites were there at that time of year. As the exodus group was making its way from the desert of Sin to Mount Horeb, the birds were also making their way across the Gulf of Suez. Although, we can see that there was still some disbelief about God among the crowd because Moses said,

> You will know that it was the LORD when he gives you meat to eat
> in the evening. (Exod 16:8)

We may wonder why the people still had some doubts after all the amazing events they had witnessed. The probable reason is that God tries to implant faith in our hearts: a trust that is not reliant on "seeing things" but a hopeful humility that believes the best of the creator without the need for him to prove himself. God can use miracles when he desires to, but he often uses providence. People sometimes confuse a miracle with providence. A miracle is a break in the chain of normal cause and effect, but providence uses the normal run of life's events to coincide with the circumstances that are affecting our lives at that point. For example, when my dad was getting married, he needed to carry some tables for the wedding reception, a distance of about two miles, and he had no vehicle and so had to carry the load on foot. He realized the job was going to take him two journeys but that would mean he was going to miss the wedding ceremony at the church. So my dad prayed, "Lord, what can I do? I need some help, please help me Lord." Just then a truck driver saw him struggling with the tables and offered to do the job for him free of charge. In those days vehicles were not on the roads like they are today, and truck drivers even less. The truck driver told my dad that he didn't usually travel on that particular street, but he fancied a change that particular day—that was an act of providence.

Of course people can disbelieve that God was involved, calling it a happy coincidence. And that was the position that the people involved in the exodus found themselves. Yes, they had seen some amazing events occur, but there was still room with each event for the people to harden their hearts against God if they wanted to, they could tell themselves that it was luck and nothing more, random chance working in their favor. Pharaoh himself had been successful in hardening his heart by selling himself a story that would enable him to continue being selfish, regardless of how many people he hurt along the way.

The crowd of people being led by Moses saw a cloud somewhere in the distance in front of them, but clouds are not uncommon, and this cloud had an eerie glow at night time, but perhaps it was a phenomenon of the desert, a bit like the aurora borealis are in the extremities of the northern and southern hemispheres. So, in a rare dispensation granted to "grumbling people," the glory of the Lord began to shine in the cloud. Sure enough, that evening the plump quails came and covered the camp. The next morning manna arrived on the ground of their camp.

The Lord was doing what he could to quench the "grumbling" of the people: he had graciously shown the people his glory and provided them with an evening meal and breakfast. The breakfast would be a feature of the time spent in Sinai, and the quail would last for some time, they also had some animals of their own they could slaughter, so considering the circumstances they had no reason for moaning. With patience and grace, the Lord tried to stop their grousing with grouse.

Chapter 23

Mineral Mines

YIELDS OF COPPER WERE not exceptional in the mines of Sinai, Egypt imported considerable quantities of the ductile metal. The mines at Serabit el-Khadim were used for mining some copper, and also the semi-precious stone turquoise that was used for Egyptian jewelry. We understand that an Egyptian mining expedition had taken place when Moses and Aaron were previously in the Serabit el-Khadim area, not too long ago. Now the children of Israel found themselves directed to that same area where God said they would worship him, as a sign to Moses, on Mount Horeb. There is a stretch of sand that lies between Serabit el-Khadim and Mount Horeb. Mount Sinai is connected to the same hill range as Serabit el-Khadim, the distance between all three mountains is not great. The sandy area, which can be clearly seen on a satellite map view, was called Rephidim by the Israelites. Strong's Concordance tells us Rephidim comes from a root word meaning "to spread" or "refresh." The Israelites used the sandy area to camp. When Egyptologist Sir Flinders Petrie examined the area he found remains of ancient settlements that workers at the mines could sleep in. No Egyptian mining expedition was taking place at the time the Israelites were in Rephidim, so these facilities could be used.

The problem that the crowd was quick to notice, and resorted to sarcasm to make their point, was that while Rephidim was a nice enough place to rest, there was no water, and human beings need water frequently. Moses heard them ask, "Did you bring us out of Egypt to die of thirst?" (Exod

17:3). They also disappointingly added, "Is Yahweh with us or not?" (Exod 17:7). Moses took the problem to the Lord, who replied,

> Walk on ahead of the people. Take with you some elders and the staff with which you struck the Nile, and go to the rock Horeb. I will stand before you. Strike the rock and water will come out of it for the people to drink. (Exod 17:5–6)

In the time of Moses, an anthropomorphic appearance of Yahweh was rare. Adam, his sons, Enoch, Noah, Abraham, and others had seen Yahweh appear among them in the form of a man, but since the days of the patriarchs these appearances had all but ceased. But in his grace the Lord would be manifest as a man and guide Moses to the exact place on Horeb where he should strike the rock for the water to spring out. Thus the Lord would show himself to the elders, who in turn could answer the skeptics among the people that they had seen Yahweh, and that, "Yes, he is with us." Although, I imagine that the appearance of Yahweh was like that of any other man, which could leave the elders to think, *This could be an ordinary man, who happens to be here.* The elders needed faith themselves, the water springing up would be the sign that Yahweh was truly among them.

Later in the book of Exodus Moses asks to actually see Yahweh in his glory, which tells us that up until now Moses had not seen Yahweh's glory, even though he had seen Yahweh. Exodus 33:11 says, "The LORD would speak to Moses face to face, as one speaks to a friend." We ought not to think it odd that God walks on earth as a man. For since ancient times, that is the picture we get in the book of Genesis. Yahweh walked on the earth that he had created, helping and guiding its early human inhabitants who were made in his image. The Father walked on earth, just as the Son walked on earth some thousands of years later—sons do what their fathers do. I walk on the earth just as my father did before me. Jesus was no different. Men found it hard to believe that Jesus was God in the flesh. "He had no beauty or majesty to attract us to him, nothing in his appearance that we should desire him" (Isa 53:2). "Then they scoffed, "He's just the carpenter's son, and we know Mary, his mother, and his brothers" (Matt 13:55 nlt).

We note that the Lord would not show himself to the crowd, but only to Moses and the elders—those who demand a sign rarely get what they demand.

The people back at the camp were not privy to the meeting with Yahweh, but they would soon see the arrival of the water, a fact that teaches us that Rephidim was not far from Mount Horeb. If we take a look at Mount

Horeb (Jabal Ghorâbi), a satellite map view will show us a wadi that has at one time been full of water. Water, in bedrock well below the surface of the earth, can be pressurized into making its way to the surface. God, who is able to see what men cannot see, knew where this water was and prepared this arrangement from long ages past. When Moses hit the rock at a certain point a fissure appeared allowing the spring of water to be released. There are still springs of water in the Sinai Peninsula. One oasis is located at Ain Umm Ahmed, where water is never lacking and local people have pumps to use the water in their households for drinking, bathing, cooking, and irrigation. In her book *A History of Sinai*, Lina Eckenstein remarks that a copious supply of good water is obtainable from a well some miles down the valley from Serabit el-Khadim.[1]

Slightly to the south of Serabit el-Khadim is the Wadi Umm Agraf. The expedition of which Flinders Petrie and Lina Eckenstein were a part of, camped at the Wadi Umm Agraf. The last three letters of agraf and the last three letters of el-Khadim, "raf" and "dim," could echo Rephidim.

Egyptian mining expeditions had a fair-sized contingent of soldiers with them as security, because there were other groups who might like to obtain the copper and turquoise that was being mined by the Egyptians and their workforce. The mine in Timna Midian had a large-scale copper industry that the Midianites and local Amalekites worked, in conjunction with the Egyptians. While the Israelites were in Rephidim a group of Amalekites had made the journey to the mine at Serabit el-Khadim. The Amalekites were not happy to see this large group of people situated there. The Egyptians had force to repel any competitors who might want to use the mine, but the Israelites looked like they might be scared away if the Amalekites started to attack the outskirts of the camp and pick off a few of the weary Israelites. Deuteronomy 25:17–18 informs us of the tactics used by the Amalekites, and today we would probably call it terrorism. Moses responded by giving orders to Joshua to select able men and form a militia for the purpose of terminating the guerrilla warfare of the Amalekites.

Combat with insurgents in hills and craggy terrain would not be an easy task, as modern armed forces know well. Moses had some considerable military experience serving with the Egyptian army during his first 40 years of life, so he would be able to pass on to Joshua strategic instructions that would help pry their Amalekite adversaries out from their cover. Also, and most importantly, God was on the side of the Israelite fighters. Moses

1. Eckenstein, *History of Sinai*, 18.

made his way to the high ground of Serabit el-Khadim, and as long as Moses held his hands aloft, the Israelite commandos had success in taking out their attackers. But if Moses let his hands rest by his side, the Israelite mission floundered. Once Moses had figured this out, he made sure his hands were held high, and Aaron and Hur gave Moses the necessary aid to make sure his arms were up. By nightfall, Joshua's men had been successful.

Moses must have felt a certain amount of physical pain that day. We can see a picture of Christ's arms being held aloft on the cross. While the arms of Jesus were held aloft on the cross the battle against the enemy of our souls was being won.

Moses was once again told to write this episode down (Exod 17:14). We can see one reason why the Lord was so insistent that Moses was the man for the job: his education, and particularly his writing abilities at a time when the alphabet-based Proto-Sinaitic script was clearly emerging as the way forward for written communication. Moses was able to succinctly relate the exodus story and also collate any oral-traditional histories or cuneiform writings that had passed through the family into the new alphabetic script—giving us the beginnings of the Bible we read today.

Chapter 24

Relatives

THE BOOKS OF GENESIS and Exodus give us enough information, if we look, to piece together the events that took place. We are told that Jethro, the priest of Midian made his way to Rephidim while Moses and the people were there. Jethro had heard of everything that God had done for the Israelites. We then hear that Jethro also brought along Zipporah, the wife of Moses, and his two sons to Rephidim. Therefore, we see that Moses had previously told his wife and family to make their way to Midian. This would have happened on the exodus journey from Marah (Bitter Lakes) towards Elim (Ayun Musa): halfway between the two resting places there is a trail to Midian and the east. The route passes through the historic Mitla Pass and then on to the town of Nekhel (where Moses and his wife Zipporah lodged on their way to Egypt). The road then leads on to the tip of the Gulf of Aqaba, from where Midian is easy to reach. The journey was about 210 miles. Jethro, who was now a priest in Midian after the death of his father Reuel, would have known the long history of the Israelites' struggle in Egypt because Moses had told him the story during the many years Moses stayed and worked with Jethro's family. Moses wanted Jethro to be briefed on what had recently happened, so Moses dispatched Zipporah and his sons Gershom and Eliezer, and probably a few men for protection, to head east and inform his in-laws what had recently occurred and how God had set the Israelites free from their enslavement in Egypt. Moses told Zipporah to tell her brother Jethro the news and then bring Jethro to the sandy stretch of land, known locally as Rephidim, which lies at the foot of the Serabit el-Khadim mine. Jethro would be familiar with the route because his family traded with the Egyptian mine supervisors at Serabit el-Khadim.

The round trip for Zipporah to arrive at Rephidim would take in 326 miles. Therefore, travelling at 20 miles a day and with two weeks of rest for Zipporah and her children at the family home in Midian, which includes preparation for Jethro and his family to make their journey, the timeframe for Zipporah and Jethro to arrive at Rephidim would be around 32 days from when Zipporah first left Moses.

Moses and the people arrived at Elim shortly after Zipporah bid them farewell. The exodus community stayed at Elim a few days and they reached the desert of Sin on the 15th day of the 2nd month. So they had been on the road 30 days when they reached the desert of Sin. There was then about 50 miles for the Israelites to travel to Serabit el-Khadim/Rephidim, which is normally a 3-day journey but the Israelites stopped and made camp 4 times between Elim and Rephidim. Moses and his entourage arrived at Rephidim and waited for Zipporah to return from her mission of reporting the news.

We may ask, why was it Zipporah who was assigned to this task? The answer seems to be, "Who better?" Jethro would welcome her with open arms and be eager to hear her news. If someone else had been dispatched to break the news then Jethro may be reticent to head to Serabit el-Khadim because it was a long journey, and plans would have to be made for it, including deputies to keep the family business running and the priesthood functioning. Plus Jethro may have thought the whole story was a trap, luring him into some sort of ambush. So Zipporah and her sons were the ideal candidates for the job.

Jethro knew the way to the mine at Serabit el-Khadim: turn left at Nekhel and follow the trail. The family had probably made the journey a number of times before, delivering their cargo of animals to the food preparation managers of the mines. Rephidim was the prearranged place for Jethro and Moses to meet, because all the parties knew where it was. Zipporah may have asked Moses how she could get to Rephidim, and he would reply, "Do not worry my wife, your brother Jethro knows the way. Bring him to me there."

Of course, Moses had another wife, which we haven't forgotten about. Did his Ethiopian wife make the original journey to Midian with him all those years ago? Perhaps she did, we can't rule it out. But she may have stayed in Egypt. Some trouble would brew a year after the exodus that centered around the Ethiopian wife of Moses, seeming to indicate that she was a new addition to the family. In which case Moses's Ethiopian wife had not seen Moses for the 40-year period he was in Midian. If she was a young bride—which did happen in those days—say about 18 years of age, and Moses was a dashing commander in the Egyptian army of about 35 years of age, then around 45 years had passed since their wedding. The Ethiopian wife would be 63 years old. What the exact story was, we don't know, but his Ethiopian wife was with him on the exodus trail. If Moses's Ethiopian wife had not seen him for some 40 years then we get to see a little of Moses's character, in as much as he searched her out in Egypt, and made sure they were together for the rest of their wedded life. How Zipporah took this we can only guess, the custom of those days did mean some men had more than one wife, and if the men had the strength and means to provide for their wives, the women themselves, as far as we know, seemed willing enough to get married.

Jethro sent one of the Hebrew men who accompanied Zipporah on ahead as a runner to let Moses know the precise time of their arrival at Rephidim. Jethro and some of his family members, along with Zipporah, Gershom, and Eliezer arrived at the prearranged meeting point of Rephidim.

The fact that all these remote places had their own names, tells us that the area was frequented by people who worked in and around the mining area; all the workers knew the place names because they would need to go to each area if they were stationed there for some reason, so it was necessary to give each area its own place name. The Israelites knew all the place names and recorded them for us.

Moses brought Jethro up to speed with what had been happening since Zipporah embarked upon her news reporting mission, and there was much to tell: manna, quail, water, and the Amalekite conflict. Jethro and Moses had a good brotherly relationship and they were overjoyed to see each other again. Jethro was pleased and very interested that God was using Moses for this special job. After all, Jethro was a priest and knew something of who God was. We can see that Moses respected Jethro's position and bowed down and kissed him.

Jethro said, "Praise be to Yahweh" (Exod 18:10). Jethro did not descend from Isaac, or even from Sarah, but descended from Abraham and Keturah's offspring. God had a plan for the Israelites, but he also works in the lives of any nation, tribe, or person who will make themselves available to him. In Acts 10:35–34 (kjv) we read, "Peter opened *his* mouth, and said, 'Of a truth I perceive that God is no respecter of persons: But in every nation he that feareth him, and worketh righteousness, is accepted with him.'" Jethro was a worker of righteousness and knew God; he was a wise man who would turn the hearts of his compatriots towards God.

Any large group of people will have disagreements, discord, and disturbance, it is the nature of human beings, we ought not, but the facts tell us that where there are humans, disputes will follow. Churches are not immune and even the early church had judgements that had to be made. The Israelites, and those with them in the wilderness, were no different. When people have a disagreement they often seek out someone who is higher in authority, this procedure is embedded in us from an early age, where we hear children sometimes say, "I'm telling my dad about you." Moses sat in the seat of the judge, we can imagine the people saying, "Okay then, let's take the matter to Moses and see what he says." While they had a few days at Rephidim, the court was able to sit, perhaps akin in vein to the modern-day *Judge Judy* on TV. Jethro saw Moses decide one case after another, with Moses saying, "Next case, please. Step forward." The disputes were basically teaching righteousness to the people. God is righteous and Moses taught the people God's laws: if something had been stolen, it must be returned. If someone had been treated disrespectfully then apologies should be made and Moses would point out why we need to respect each other. Jethro saw that Moses was teaching what all human beings should do: do to others as you yourself would have them do to you.

Jethro could see what was happening so gave Moses some valuable advice. The work was too heavy for Moses alone, he needed to delegate. Jethro told Moses to appoint trustworthy men as judges. Moses had more pressing matters to attend to—he was meeting with God and learning more of what God was doing with the Israelites, particularly as their plan was to head towards their promised land. Moses also had the job of writing that he needed to attend to. Jethro pointed out something that the apostles in Acts 6:2 noted: "It would not be right for us to neglect the ministry of the word of God in order to wait on tables." Moses was in a similar position and Jethro pointed it out.

This is a clear lesson of how God gives us our own work to do. God could have told Moses himself, but the Lord delegated the work to Jethro. He knew that Jethro had the wisdom and experience to guide Moses in this matter. God took a step back and allowed men to relay his will to each other. God doesn't do everything for us: we have to rise to the challenge ourselves. Adam was given the job of naming all the animals he saw, God could have done it but he wants us to add our own mark on his creation. A mother may teach her child how to paint a picture of a house, the parent could do the job herself, but that wouldn't help society move forward. God, in a similar way, wants us to use the creative abilities that he has placed in us. We are all a part of God's creation and if we all played our part as he intended, our lives would be different.

Here, we see a Midian priest guiding the fledgling Israelite nation. Jethro's advice to Moses may have had a long-term effect on the Israelite community—we can see the beginnings of the judges that would later rule in Israel.

Chapter 25

Time

WHEN WE TAKE A step back we can sometimes see a larger picture. So let us have a think about the timing of what was taking place in and around the events of the exodus.

The Egyptian New Year began in the summer. But God wanted the Israelites to make the month of Abib their first month (Exod 12:2, 13:4). The month of Abib begins around the time of the spring equinox. (The name "Abib" changed to "Nisan" around the time of the Babylonian exile.) The name Abib was related to the ripeness of the barley crop, when the crop was in ear and the new moon appeared it was said to be the season of spring. That was the beginning of the month of Abib. Abib can be spelled as Aviv too (the well known city in Israel called Tel Aviv means "hill of spring.")

According to the Hebrew text of Exodus 9:31, when the Egyptian barley crop was devastated by the plague of hail, the barley was in abib. The grain was in bloom or was "in the ear," in a state of abib. When the new moon was seen after the barley was in ear, this was the point when the month of Abib started. The Egyptians and the Hebrews had lunar months. We can see the word "moon" in the word "month," a month relates to the phases of the moon. A lunar month lasts an average of 29.53 days. So from one year to the next, the months would slowly slip backward compared to the solar year and a leap month would be added in to make sure the seasons coincided correctly with their calendar year, which was important for agriculture. The Egyptians split their month up into three *decans* of 10 days each, which was their 10-day week. The Israelites would have to work within the Egyptian system because they were forced to do so. The early Mesopotamian week was 7 days long. Abraham came from Mesopotamia and descended from Adam, so the 7-day week would be familiar to him and to his descendants.

The Passover meal began in the "evening" of the 14th day of Abib (Nisan). The "evening" means the day had just begun: the Hebrews counted a day from evening (sundown) to evening the next day, thus incorporating two Roman calendar days. Jesus ate the Passover meal with his disciples at the beginning of 14th Nisan. (In the Roman Julian calendar this was still the evening of Thursday, April 2, 33 AD—what Christians celebrate as Maundy Thursday.) Jesus died on the same day: on 14th Nisan at about 3:00 pm in the afternoon. (In the Julian calendar this was the afternoon of Friday, April 3, 33 AD—what Christians remember as Good Friday.) So Jesus was able to eat the Passover meal with his disciples at the beginning of 14th Nisan and he died later on that same day.

The Israelites do not have names for the days of the week, except the Sabbath. The other days are referred to as numbers, day one or day two, etc. If we extend both the Rabbinic and Julian calendars backwards, we notice that when the original Passover occurred in 1406 BC the days 14th and 15th Abib were also the 6th day (Friday) and Sabbath (Saturday). Jesus died on Good Friday and was in the tomb during the Sabbath.

However, we have to say that the days of the week are not always certain when it comes to calendars. Modern astronomers are able to work out when a new moon occurred, so we have a good idea when the start of a month began, but what day of the week the Hebrews were in is not so easy to calculate.

The Julian calendar calculated a year to be 365.25 days in length. (The Egyptian year was also the same length.) Julius Caesar introduced the Julian calendar to the Roman world in 46 BC, even though Greek astronomers, up to 100 years prior, knew that a year wasn't quite that long. The Julian calendar meant a day would be lost every 128 years. Pope Gregory in 1582 AD corrected the slight error by introducing a year that was 365.2425 days long: making a difference of 10 minutes 48 seconds per year. It doesn't sound like much, but over long stretches of time the new length of the year proved to be far more accurate. That's why we have the Gregorian calendar these days. But even so, a day is still lost, but only once in every 3,300 years.

Astronomers tend not to use the regular calendar because they need a system that is accurate for their calculations, so they use a "day count" method. Rather than counting solar years or lunar months, astronomers count the days themselves. They name each day since January 1, 4713 BC with a number. For example January 1, 4713 BC is called "0," the following day, January 2, 4713 BC is called "1," and so on. The system is called Julian Day Numbers. We can look back with confidence when we attribute to each day its own specific number. The number given for the exodus on 14th Abib 1406 BC is 1,207,973. (We can check this date because we know when the new moon first began to show around the spring equinox, which would be the beginning of the month of Abib.) If we check the date that Jesus died on the cross, April 3, 33AD (14th Nisan/Abib 33 AD), the Julian Day Number is 1,733,204. Now if we take the number of days between those two Julian Day Numbers we will arrive at the number of days between the first Passover and the crucifixion, the number is 525,231 days, a number divisible by 7. We can also see there were 75,033 weeks between the Passover and the crucifixion. Furthermore and interestingly we see that Julian Day Number 1,207,973 (14th Abib 1406 BC) was a particular day of the week. We can find out which day by dividing the number of days between the Passover and crucifixion. So if we think that day 1,207,973 (14th Nisan 1406 BC) might be a Friday, we can add the 525,231 days to check, and because the 525,231 days are divisible by 7, we find we are correct in supposing 14th Abib 1406 BC was a Friday too.

We can now turn our attention once more to Exodus 12:40 (kjv): "Now the sojourning of the children of Israel, who dwelt in Egypt, was four hundred and thirty years." We should note, the wording, "the sojourning" of the children of Israel, who dwelt in Egypt; that is, the sojourning of the Israelite nation. The word "sojourning" includes the first journey made by Abraham from the city of Ur, his journeys in Canaan and Egypt, his grandson Jacob's journey to Paddan Aram in northern Mesopotamia, and the family's final journey south into Egypt. The "sojourning" included all of these previous journeys, because in Egypt the children of Israel did not sojourn—they were given a location: Goshen. Hence, the Scripture says, "the sojourning of the children of Israel, who 'dwelt' in Egypt." The root of the Hebrew word used for "sojourning" can also be used for "dwellings" or "settlements" so we could think of Exodus 12:40 meaning "The length of time throughout all the places Abraham's family dwelt from when he first set out totalled 430 years."

Let us also be careful about the phrase "children of Israel." This was a name for them as a nation, which included their roots back to Abraham, not only the actual "children" or "offspring" of Israel (or of Jacob as he was also known), because Jacob himself went to Egypt and he can be included in the phrase "children of Israel." The narrative is telling us that from the time Abraham left his native country and began the sojourning, to the release of his posterity from enslavement in Egypt, totalled 430 years. The Septuagint includes Canaan as well, stating in Exodus 12:40, "Now the residence of the sons of Israel during which they dwelt in the land, Egypt, and in the land of Canaan was four hundred and thirty years." The term "children of Israel" includes the people before Jacob too (i.e., Isaac and Abraham). The NIV translates the term "children of Israel" as the "Israelite people" and the Samaritan Pentateuch states, "the sojourning of the children of Israel and their fathers, who dwelt in Canaan and in Egypt, [was] four hundred and thirty years." Both of the Jewish Talmuds agree, stating, "in Egypt, and in the rest of the lands." The time period of 430 years began from the promise made to Abraham, as the Apostle Paul explains in Galatians 3:17. The verse following Exodus 12:40 remarks that the 430 years was "to the very day." That phrase reveals that Abraham left the city of Ur on the 14th of the month of Abib 1836 BC, the Julian Day Number for that day is 1,050,928, which the Julian Day and Civil Date Calculator inform us was also a Friday.[1]

We also have to ask the question, were Jacob's descendants following a 7-day week while they were in Egypt? They were not particularly commanded to have a 7-day week prior to the exodus, nor were they commanded to hold a Sabbath day of rest. We don't read of the Sabbath in the Bible until we get to the book of Exodus. We do read in the book of Genesis that God rested on the 7th day, and Adam and his descendants most probably followed God's example, because Yahweh had spoken to Adam about it and set the process of a 7-day week for humanity in motion. It's right and proper to take a day off. We can't keep on working one day after the other without a break. We can see a little of why God broke down the narrative of the creation of the universe into 7 days—humans needed to follow God's example. Although the length of a day for God and the length of a day for us may differ enormously, the lesson is still there for us to apply to ourselves.

God didn't "command" Adam and his descendants to take a break, the Lord led by example. Yahweh was someone whom Adam would want to emulate, so the 7-day week was a part of Adam's life as well as getting passed on to the surrounding Mesopotamian people. We can see that Cain and Abel took time off work to present Yahweh with a gift or offering (Gen

1. Numerical, "Julian Day."

4:3–4). Therefore, they did not work every day. The story of Noah also has a number of allusions to 7 days. And the word "week" is actually mentioned in Genesis 29:27–28 regarding Jacob's wife Leah completing her bridal week. Leah and Jacob were in northern Mesopotamia at the time. The Hebrew word mentioned in regard to Leah and Jacob's week is *shabua*, which means a heptad: a group of 7.

At the other end of the Fertile Crescent we find that the Egyptians did not keep a single day in 7 special. As we have seen, they didn't even have a 7-day week. The early Mesopotamians did have a 7-day week, and many people have debated just why that is the case. One school of thought supposes that the Mesopotamians chose 7 days for a week because of the 7 moving celestial bodies we can see with the naked eye: the Sun, Moon, Mars, Mercury, Jupiter, Venus, and Saturn. (We call the days of the week after those names: Sun for Sunday, Moon for Monday, and Saturn for Saturday. Tuesday, Wednesday, Thursday, and Friday have been replaced in English with the names of Germanic/Norse deities: *Tiw* for Tuesday, *Woden* for Wednesday, *Thor* for Thursday, and *Freya* for Friday. *Tiw* was equated with Mars, which is why in French Tuesday is called *Mardi* and in Spanish it's called *Martes*.) Another viewpoint is that a lunar month can be divided up into 4 quarters of 7 days each. Well, almost, but it doesn't quite work out.

The Bible offers another explanation as to why the Mesopotamians may have had a 7-day week. We know that Yahweh was active in southern Mesopotamia because he brought water to the area and planted a garden. He explained to the man in charge of the garden that he had created the universe in 7 days. The man and his children, to whom Yahweh imparted this information, were held in high esteem in Mesopotamia because of their long lives, strength, and wisdom. From this we understand that the Mesopotamians learned of the 7-day week through Adam and his offspring. God spoke to the hearts of all early humans, but they had begun to go their own way, as we are told in Ecclesiastes 7:29, "God created mankind upright, but they have gone in search of many schemes." So God highlighted his message to us through Adam and his offspring, the 7-day week being a small part of that message.

God also wrote of the importance of the indivisible number 7 in the skies. Psalm 19:1–4 explains that the night-time sky has a voice:

> The heavens declare the glory of God;
>> the skies proclaim the work of his hands.
> Day after day they pour forth speech;
>> night after night they display knowledge.

There is no speech or language where their voice is not heard.

Their voice goes out into all the earth, their words to the ends of the world.

Adam's son Seth is reputed by Josephus to have been a fine astronomer and so he would have noted the 7 wandering celestial bodies. Names were given to these travelling lights in the sky and a temptation arose for subsequent generations to think of these physical spheres as gods, or as representing celestial beings. The Bible explains that though men have gods ruling their lives there is in fact only one true God. Even today people will try to "read the stars," and horoscopes are written that are thought to rule over certain aspects of people's lives.

The first book of the Bible emphasizes the number 7 with the creative days, and the last book of the Bible stresses the number 7 with the 7 lampstands, 7 stars, 7 churches, 7 seals, etc. Perhaps, the fact that God specifically commanded a 7th day of rest to the group of people leaving Egypt, means that both the 7-day week and the 7th day of rest had been lost and needed to be reinstated. So, God wrote it in stone—something we may have happen in our own lives from time to time: we fail to do what is correct concerning a certain issue, so God gives us a reminder that we will never forget.

We first heard about a day of rest in Genesis 2:3, but the trail for the Sabbath day seems to go cold. The liberated Israelites were told to "Remember the Sabbath day," as if somewhere along the line a day of rest had been lost and they needed to remember it and start applying it to their lives once more. In the story of the exodus we can see God looking for an opportunity to reinstate the 7-day week, and finding one.

The date of reaching the desert of Sin was the 15th day of the 2nd month. The desert of Sin is where the community grumbled against Moses and Aaron because they were worried about supplies of food. The Lord seems to have seized this opportunity to reintroduce the 7-day week. He promises to send food from the skies for the Israelites but there is a proviso—they can only gather this food for 6 days, on the 7th day they cannot gather the food because there won't be any food to gather. They must collect enough on the 6th day for the 7th day too. But even so, some of the people (who did not seem familiar with this 7th-day-of- rest principle) went out to gather the food on the 7th day but found no food to collect. So the 1st day that food appeared for them would be "day one." The people reached the desert of Sin on the 15th day on the 2nd month: the company of people were hungry on their journey from Elim to the desert of Sin so the Lord said that evening they would eat meat. If the month of Abib only had 29 days that year, which is possible, because originally there was no fixed calendar, each month began anew, the leaders would determine whether the month would be 29 or 30 days. Lunar months can be slightly shorter or longer depending on where the moon is in its orbit. So if the 15th day of the 2nd month is specifically mentioned in the book of Exodus for us to note that it was the 1st day of meat and manna, that would make the day a Sunday (1st day of the week according to its Julian Day Number). So this could have been the opportunity that God was looking for to reintroduce the 7-day week for the Israelite community.

In Leviticus chapter 23 (kjv) the LORD tells us when the feast days should take place. The significance of the feast days is worthy for us to note. "In the fourteenth day of the first month at evening is the LORD's Passover." In other words the feast will begin at the start of the day on 14th Abib. (In Genesis chapter 1 the day starts in the evening: "And there was evening, and there was morning—the first day." So the evening was the beginning of the day for the Israelites.) The Passover date coincides with the death of Jesus who died on 14th Abib/Nisan.

The next feast occurs the following day: "On the fifteenth day of that month the LORD's Festival of Unleavened Bread begins" (Lev 23:6), the 15th Abib. That day was a special Sabbath, regardless of what day of the week it was, where no servile work was done. Later when Israel was a nation in their own country, a special Sabbath would sometimes coincide with the 7th-day Sabbath, and when two Sabbaths conjoined, the day would be called a "high day." John describes this occurrence in his Gospel, "the bodies would not remain on the cross on the Sabbath (for that Sabbath was a high day)" (John 19:31). The Feast of Unleavened Bread coincides with Jesus resting in the tomb on 15th Abib/Nisan.

On the following day, the 16th Abib, the first sheaf of harvest was to be waved by the priest before the LORD, it was the day after the special Sabbath and called the First Fruits. The day 16th Abib/Nisan in 33 AD was when Jesus rose from the dead—Jesus was the first fruits of us all, because, as the Bible teaches, one day we will all rise from the dead.

Leviticus 23 also points out that from the 16th Abib/Nisan, 50 days are to be counted when another wave offering is to be made, the day would also be a special Sabbath. In 49 days there are 7 weeks. The 50th day means a completion of seven sevens. What is known as the Feast of Weeks took place on the 50th day. The Greek word for fiftieth is *pentecost*. On the

50th day after the resurrection of Jesus the Holy Spirit descended upon the disciples, what Christians celebrate as the Day of Pentecost.

So, as the daylight began to shine, about 12 hours into the 14th day of the month of Abib, the Israelites set out from Egypt on their journey. The day the Israelites were set free would be the same date on which Jesus would later die. The prophet Joel tells us that, "a day of darkness and gloom, a day of clouds and blackness" (Joel 2:2), would come, and at the end of the chapter, that "the sun will be turned to darkness and the moon to blood." The apostle Peter reminded the crowd of Joel's prophecy when he spoke to them on the Day of Pentecost. Mark 15:33 relates that on the day Jesus died, "When it was noon, darkness came over the whole land until three in the afternoon." So it looks like, the day Jesus died the sky was overcast with dark clouds. By evening time when the moon arose, the sky had cleared, and interestingly, NASA has on record a partial lunar eclipse for April 3, 33 AD, which would give a red tinge to the appearance of the moon. A lunar eclipse can occur only when the moon is full and in the middle of the month. The Lord was specific with Moses about the 14th day of the month, Christ died on 14th Nisan, so at moonrise as the 15th Nisan began the moon would be full.

Fourteen days into the month of Abib the Israelites were on the move. On the 1st day they travelled 20 miles to Succoth, which would be reached towards the end of the 14th Abib. When the evening came the 15th Abib would begin, and the people would bake their unleavened bread for their evening meal: the 15th Abib is the celebration of Unleavened Bread. On the morning of the 2nd day they travelled 9 miles to Etham. On the 3rd day they strategically returned northwards for 24 miles, following the western shoreline of the freshwater lakes, almost reaching Migdol. On the 4th day they passed through the Sea of Reeds and found themselves on the east side of the freshwater lakes and heading 55 miles south for 3 days. Feeling thirsty, they came to Marah.

Their time at Marah was short. They did not stay too long, and continued their march, partly because Zipporah and a few others had to make a left turn, heading for Midian. The rest of the troupe headed 30 miles south, which is a long hike, but worth the effort to reach Elim and its idyllic setting. The community would probably have stayed at Elim for a few days rest. (The area was pleasant and a longer rest after all their travelling would be helpful.) We could also remember that the Israelites worked hard while enslaved in Egypt, they were good workers and that is one of the reasons why Pharaoh was loathe to lose them, so the people's fitness for the long journeys would not be a problem. They were probably fitter than people in the modern world by some measure.

Once refreshed, the people left Elim for the next camp, which was along the east coast of the Gulf of Suez (Red Sea). The journey lasted 25 miles and was done in one leg. Camp was set up at the Gulf of Suez coast and the assembly probably stayed there a few days. The company of people reached the desert of Sin on the 15th day of the 2nd month: the month of Ziv. The community had been on the road for 31 days since the exodus began.

The next leg was to Dophkah, a journey of 30 miles from the desert of Sin. Most able-bodied people have a walking pace that feels comfortable at around 3 miles per hour, although we can walk at a faster pace without much trouble. Exodus 13:18 (nasb) says, "the sons of Israel went up in martial array from the land of Egypt," which gives us the picture of an army marching. But let us say the exodus crowd was moving along at 3 mph—there were about 13.5 hours of daylight in that area at that time of year, and they also had the pillar of cloud by day and fire by night, which enabled them to travel by day or night (Exod 13:21). So let us suppose that at daybreak (approximately 5:00 am) they started to pack their personal effects, a task that may have taken an hour to complete, then travelling at a pace of 3 mph they would be able to cover 30 miles in 10 hours. If they set out at 6:00 am they would arrive at Dophkah at 5:00 pm, which includes two rest breaks of 30 minutes each. They could then set up camp for the evening with the remaining sunlight that would begin to set at about 6:30 pm. Any stragglers who arrived later would have some incandescent light from the pillar of fire, plus a nearly full moon. The smoke from the pillar seems to have a similar quality to smoke from a furnace: in daylight the pillar appears as smoke rising upwards but at night time we see there is actually heat in the smoke which is able to give a glow of light.

The distance from Dophkah to Rephidim was less than 20 miles, but a stop along the route at a place Numbers 33:13 calls Alush, was preferable because of the hard terrain. The people's arrival at Rephidim from the desert of Sin would have taken 3 days with no rest days between overnight stops: a distance of 50 miles, enabling the Israelites to arrive at Rephidim on day 34 after the exodus began. The Amalekites were quick to start picking off the weary stragglers among the exodus crowd, which would have happened on day 34 because Deuteronomy 25:17–18 (nasb) states,

> Remember what Amalek did to you . . . how he met you along the
> way and attacked among you all the stragglers at your rear when
> you were faint and weary.

The insight we gain from this Scripture is that the Israelites had not quite completed their journey to Rephidim but were attacked by the Amalekites who used guerrilla hit-and-run tactics aimed towards the rear of the exodus travellers. The Amalekite threat was quickly dealt with the following day, being the 35th day.

Around the 39th day Jethro and his family arrived. Some days of legal duties and appointing of judges took place and then on the 47th day after the exodus the camp was moved the short 3 or 4 miles to the desert of Sinai: a short stretch of sheltered sand alongside Mount Horeb and Mount Sinai. Mount Serabit el-Khadim was about 4 miles further west, but in the same mountain range.

As we read through the book of Exodus we begin to get the feeling that the author wants us to take note of the timeline because the days of particular months are mentioned. The first verse of Exodus chapter 19 is one of those occasions: "In the third month . . . on the very day," we are asked to log this 1st day of the 3rd month because, presumably it's worthy of note. Arrival in the desert of Sinai occurred on the 47th day. (Working on 29 days for the month of Abib [the 1st month], and 30 days for the month of Ziv [the 2nd month], we can understand that the 47th day was the arrival at the desert of Sinai—the first day of the month of Sivan [the 3rd month].) The next time period we are asked to notice is when the LORD tells Moses:

> Go to the people and consecrate them today and tomorrow. Have
> them wash their clothes and be ready by the third day, because on
> that day the LORD will come down on Mount Sinai in the sight of
> all the people. (Exod 19:10–11)

We are asked to note a 3-day period. Arrival at basecamp in the sandy area known locally as the desert of Sinai occurred on the 47th day. On the 48th day while the people organized their camp, Moses ascended the mountain, which was not a high mountain and could be accessed by a fit man without too much trouble. Moses was 80 years old but he was a long-liver and still had some strength from Adam's stock in his legs.

The strength and long years began to dissipate as time went on but Moses, Aaron, Caleb, Joshua, and a number of others still had access to that strength. God had said that his Spirit would not always strive with Adam's line, and his days would be 120. Moses lived to be that age, but that looks to be a turning point and we find that King David had a regular lifespan. But Moses was able to negotiate the mountain range in the Serabit el-Khadim area without struggle. On that 48th day Moses had woken and saw that the pillar of cloud that had led the Israelites to the desert of Sinai had now moved higher up onto the mountain. Mineworkers periodically frequented the area and called this particular mountain Sinai. Moses needed to find out what was going to happen next so he made his way to the cloud. The LORD told Moses what was on his heart. He wanted the Israelite nation to be his treasured possession but they needed to obey him, but would they? By evening Moses was back at basecamp, and the next day (the 49th) called an assembly of the elders and put Yahweh's proposal to the representatives of the people, who each consulted their constituents and all parties responded with an affirmation that they were willing to obey and do everything the LORD says.

> The people all responded together, "We will do everything the LORD has said." (Exod 19:8)

So the following day (the 50th) Moses made his way back up the mountain and informed Yahweh of the people's response, which is when the LORD tells Moses about the 3 days. The LORD tells Moses that on the 3rd day he will get closer to the people, but the people must not try to push through and see him. God is good and having bad men push through to try to smash their way into heaven was never going to work. The 3rd day would fall on the 52nd day after the Passover but the 50th day after the 16th of Abib—equating to the Day of Pentecost.

The morning began with thick cloud, lightening, and thunder, which is not particularly supernatural but quite alarming. The Israelites were about to have the fear of God put into them a little further by hearing a trumpet sound too. Moses led the people away from the camp towards the foot of the mountain. The pillar of cloud had started to envelope the whole mountain and smoke like that from a furnace rose from it. The trumpet started to slowly crescendo until Moses spoke and the LORD answered him. The LORD called for Moses to ascend the mountain, which he did, and by now he knew the quickest route up and probably made short work of it. The LORD emphasized that the people were not to actually set foot on the mountain but they could watch and listen. But Aaron would be allowed to ascend the mountain with Moses. So Moses descended the mountain and repeated the warning to the people telling them not to try and break through.

Chapter 26

God Speaks

WHEN MOSES FIRST CLIMBED Mount Sinai, God told him to pass on a message to the fledgling nation of Israel.

> Tell the people of Israel: "You yourselves have seen what I did to Egypt, and how I carried you on eagles' wings and brought you to myself." (Exod 19:3–4)

We gain some insight from this message of the way the Lord likes to communicate to us. The simile of the "eagles' wings" is poetic, illustrative, and loving. The Israelites' flight out of Egypt was swift like the flight of an eagle. Their enemy even tried to pursue them but could not catch up with them, because God had given the people of the exodus wings. We ought to bear in mind when reading the Scriptures that God enjoys using these poetic figures of speech and remember that he has creative flair. He prefers to talk to us in such a way, but sometimes the Lord has to tell people in a plain fashion, ensuring there is no room for an unscrupulous person to sneak through a loophole with intrigue. Jesus also enjoyed using creative similes but we read that sometimes they could not grasp his figures of speech, "So then he told them plainly" (John 11:14).

The morning of the 50th day God spoke in a direct manner to the whole community. God's first communication to the people was to introduce himself, much like people do when first meeting. God had previously introduced himself to Abraham at the city of Ur, and later on Isaac got to know the Lord in Canaan. God also made himself known to Jacob in a dream and Moses in a burning bush, now he made himself known to the people who had come out of Egypt. "I am Yahweh your God who brought you out of Egypt, out of the land of slavery" (Exod 20:2). God makes this point plainly: it wasn't lucky chance. It was Yahweh who engineered the process of emancipation for the slaves in Egypt—in case any of them were still wondering! The people knew there had been a cloud some way ahead of them, but they followed Moses, who in turn followed the cloud. The crowd must have asked among themselves, "What is that cloud?" "Is it a natural occurrence or is it really Yahweh's presence, as Moses says it is?" Now, the people were privileged to hear God speak and were no longer in any doubt about who helped them escape the clutches of slavery.

The Lord waited until Moses was down among the people before speaking. He spoke from Mount Sinai, so the people heard a voice but saw no form. The voice caused consternation and alarm among the people who were near to panic, but not unnerved enough to fail to comprehend what the voice was actually saying. Moses calmed the people by telling them they were having fear put into them for their own good.

That morning the Lord spoke briefly and to the point. Ten points actually, in what theologians call the Decalogue or what most people know as the Ten Commandments:

1. "Have no other gods before me." There are lots of other gods "out there" that would dearly love to snap up this liberated young nation, they will make all sorts of promises about freedom, but what they offer as freedom turns out to be slavery. Yahweh has shown that he is the only God who truly cares about the people's freedom by setting them free from slavery in Egypt—Moses did not make the first move, God approached Moses and began the process. God cares that we are free, it is the way we are meant to live.

2. "Do not make a graven image." The Israelites may not have realized it but they were in great danger of losing their newly found freedom. When an object commands more attention than it actually deserves, the edges of slavery start to appear—a truth that still holds good in the modern world. The Israelites were being taught that the invisible God who made all that is visible cannot be contained. The Lord graciously allows us to see different aspects of himself as he desires, but we ought not to think he is a part of this universe.

3. "Do not misuse the name of the LORD." The community of people who stood and listened to the Lord's voice were told not to use the name

of Yahweh flippantly because it would imply that Yahweh is really not to be thought of as the powerful Almighty, but someone whose name can be slung around by humans who are angry or frustrated or simply trying to score points in a dispute with their neighbors. Language has been given to us as a means of expressing our thoughts and ideas, it is not meant for profanity or swearing, something that Jesus highlighted when he said, "All you need to say is 'Yes' or 'No'" (Matt 5:37).

4. "Remember the Sabbath day." A few verses further on, in Exodus 23:12, we have a little more explanation on the reasoning behind the 7th day of no work: "so that the slave born in your household and the foreigner living among you may be refreshed." Unscrupulous managers would have their workforce toil each and every day if they could. The Israelites themselves may have been in this position as slaves in Egypt, but the Israelites were not to treat their employees in that manner. God had recently reinstated the 7-day week and the day of rest within it. Where God had once led by example he now enforces the "weekly day-off" rule. The human population of this time period in the southern area of the Fertile Crescent had failed to follow God's lead where taking one rest day in seven was concerned so God found himself in the position of enforcing the people to enjoy themselves. After all, the Sabbath was made for man, not man for the Sabbath, as Jesus so succinctly put it. The trouble with issuing a command about a day of rest meant that the opportunity to get far too fastidious about what constitutes work could arise, a position that the religious elite found themselves in at the time of Jesus's ministry.

5. "Honor your father and mother." To the people among the crowd with an open and soft heart these ten qualities that Yahweh is proclaiming go without saying. But God is vocalizing them so that people are without excuse: not all humans have a soft heart, so the laying down of laws in a legislative manner enables society to be protected. Each family unit is a cell within society's larger body. If someone fails to take care of their aged parents, court proceedings may ensue, thereby helping to uphold society's cell-like structure. Our parents look after us while we are young, so when they are older it is the turn of the offspring to make sure their parents are cared for. Paul, in Ephesians 6:1–3 uses this command to also remind children of their duty to be obedient, which the command also covers because "honor" is a comprehensive word.

6. "You shall not murder." With this command we enter into what people know as the "Thou shalt nots." Christianity has sometimes been ridiculed because it is supposed to be a religion of "don't do this" and "don't do that." But the way the Lord has phrased these commands makes them far from being restrictive. If someone is going to dictate a command to us, we are far better off receiving a negative command such as, "Don't skateboard in the pedestrianized area of town," than a positive command such as "Always skateboard in the pedestrianized area of town." What? I can hardly skateboard at all, and what about my elderly mother? That means she won't ever be able to go into town. Positive commands are far more restrictive than negative commands. If a small slice of pie is being kept for a latecomer, and the cook says, "Don't eat that small slice of pie I've marked out because we are saving it for Charlotte who will be arriving later," we may ask if we can eat any of the rest of the pie. And the cook may say, "Yes, you can eat the rest of whole pie if you want to, but don't eat that little slice." Not unlike the garden of Eden scenario where Adam and Eve were free to eat from all the many and varied fruit trees, except one. "You shall not murder!" Well, that's good, because I don't want to murder anyone.

7. "You shall not commit adultery." This law is another law that helps preserve the whole body of people. If some percentage of cells in a person's physical body are damaged, the body should be able to heal itself, but if a whole host of cells are damaged, the body itself would be in danger. Each family unit being a cell in the structure of a nation means that each family within it contributes to the shape of the society. If adultery occurs, family units are often wrecked and blown apart which will have an effect upon the whole of the social order. God expects us to keep our word, we are made in his image and he is solid and trustworthy, human beings are made to reflect God's image. We sink low when we break faith with our wives or husbands, not only will our unfaithfulness be intensely painful for those we hurt but we also make a contribution to the breakdown of society itself—something the serpent is extremely interested in. God loves order, and faithfulness is built into the fabric of the universe, if we want to fit into creation as God intends us to, then keeping our behavior orderly, faithful, and trustworthy is obligatory. The Bible sometimes talks of "worthless fellows." These "worthless" people have somehow mislaid their value. They had a precious soul but have failed to tend to it. The

Scriptures warn us not to lose our souls: "For what shall it profit a man, if he shall gain the whole world, and lose his own soul?" (Mark 8:36 kjv).

8. "You shall not steal." A man can work long and hard shaping a metal or stone tool that will help him and his family live more comfortably in their surroundings. The tool belongs to him, and is what we know as "private property." If someone, who does not want to work hard shaping a tool steals the implement from its original owner, the owner has legal recourse available to him because of this command. Theft is not for those who follow God. The animal kingdom has its share of thieves, including hyenas, gulls, monkeys, dogs, and the fox, and we don't blame them because this world is their home, it's the way they live. But we are taught not to "bite and devour each other," and to "watch out or you will be destroyed by each other" (Gal 5:15). Worldliness is not for the righteous. Humanity is made in God's image and should not sink to the ways of this world. Paul in the New Testament exhorts those who have been stealing to steal no longer, but to work, doing something useful with their own hands, that they may have something to share with those in need (Eph 4:28).

9. "You shall not give false testimony against your neighbor." In a court of law such as Moses had recently been holding to decide disputes among the people, falsifying evidence to defame or convict another person is hereby condemned outright. The intentional act of swearing a false oath in a judicial process is called perjury. Justice must prevail. False witnesses rose up against Jesus in his trial: "The chief priests and the whole Sanhedrin were looking for false evidence against Jesus so that they could put him to death" (Matt 26:59). What holds true in court is also the standard for daily life. If your boss asks you to tell someone he's out of the office when he's actually in the office, a decision has to be made whether to follow God's directive or your manager's. Righteous people should be known as people of truth. Truth is the measure by which we stand or fall. People have sometimes found themselves in trouble because of their decision to speak only the truth, and yet those people reveal themselves to be trustworthy people made in God's image because there is no falsehood in God.

10. "You shall not covet." This command deals with a person's inner being, it goes straight to the heart of a corrupt human spirit. We can look on

this command as a little inside information from the Lord on how to combat the enemy of our souls. The serpent had used a covetous desire when targeting Eve in the garden of Eden. "When the woman saw that the fruit of the tree was good for food and pleasing to the eye, and also desirable for gaining wisdom" (Gen 3:6). Cain also wanted something his brother Abel had, namely, the favorable reaction from Yahweh. But he did not receive what his brother had and was downcast, which eventually led to murder. There are other examples in Scripture: King Saul was galled by the refrain of the girl singers, "Saul has slain his thousands, and David his tens of thousands" (1 Sam 18:7). The king let the jealousy fester, and the evil grew. In due course he threw a spear at David in an attempt to kill him. The spear Saul wielded should have been aimed at his own inner temptations and he ought to have rejoiced that David had helped rescue Israel against her enemies. But the covetous nature of desiring praise equal, or above, that of David, overcame him. Saul did not manage to pierce David through, but he did end up falling on his own sword and piercing himself through. The Hebrews of the New Testament were taught a similar message to the Hebrews of the Old Testament: "be content with such things as you have" (Heb 13:5 nkjv), and thereby eradicate the corrupting influence of covetousness.

The voice from the smoking mountain stopped. The people remained at a distance.

Chapter 27

Etching the Law on Men's Hearts

AFTER THE VOICE FROM the mountain had finished speaking, the people had a chance to regain their equilibrium, and they approached Moses. Hearing Yahweh speak from heaven had been an ordeal for the people—they thought they would die—so they requested that Moses speak to them himself rather than having the trauma of hearing God speak to them. Moses knew Yahweh fairly well at this point and was aware that God is love, and would only cause the people consternation for an important reason, similar to a parent who is keen to see their children grow straight and true. Moses told the people not to be fearful: there was a reason why they were allowed to hear the voice. Moses was also talking to himself, as the people's leader he needed to muster up his own courage. Exodus 19:16 states that "Everyone in the camp trembled." That includes Moses too, as he was in the camp. The New Testament picks up on this fact in Hebrews 12:21: "The sight was so terrifying that Moses said, 'I am trembling with fear.'"

The Lord had laid down his 10-point manifesto for the people and did not intend to speak aloud to them further. The 10 decrees that the Israelites had just heard were—and still are—good for all men and women in all times of history. The voice of God speaking aloud from heaven to the earth is a rare occurrence. God chose the Sinai Desert in the late 1400s BC to proclaim his laws, not only to the Israelites but to all humanity. We can view the people gathered there as witnesses that God chose to relay the 10 laws to the rest of humanity. The first 3 laws concentrate on loving God, the following 6 on loving your neighbor, and the 10th command on enjoying a peaceful life. These are the laws of God that he spoke, and would also soon inscribe on stone. There would be other regulations laid down in the book of Exodus that pertained to the localized situation the Israelites found themselves in, but the Ten Commandments stand firm.

Moses left the people and made his way towards the dense smoke. The people looked on, still amazed at the day's proceedings. Moses located Yahweh and we are privy to what was said between them because Moses wrote it down as we are told in Exodus 24:4. On their first encounter after the pronouncement of the Decalogue, Yahweh told Moses to tell the Israelites, "You can see that I have spoken to you from heaven" (Exod 20:22). This is interesting, and means we ought not to think that "heaven" is billions of miles hence. Heaven is actually quite close to us. Celtic Christians noted that there appears to be points in the infrastructure of the material universe where the walls weaken and heaven is able to poke through. The name they had for this phenomenon was "thin places." The backdrop of this world can tear, perhaps similar to a theater backdrop with scenery painted on it at the rear of a stage, the backdrop can rip and people can see through to the backstage area where the actors reside. This space-time world we all live in seems to be a backdrop that is projected from the center of reality, the fabric of the universe is not itself the center of reality, that lies elsewhere. Paul told the Athenians that "he is not far from any one of us. 'For in him we live and move and have our being'" (Acts 17:27–28). Paul also told us to

> Fix our eyes not on what is seen, but on what is unseen, for what is
> seen is temporary, but what is unseen is eternal. (2 Cor 4:18)

God and heaven are unseen—this understanding of heaven ties in well with the "string theory" that physicists have been studying for the last few years. The physical universe we all experience appears to be a "projection" from an underlying base.

Then Yahweh told Moses not to make elaborate altars, but to make altars from earth or natural stones, not stones that have been ornately chiseled—keep the process simple using God's handiwork and not man's. God provides what is needed.

One more thing! "Don't use steps to get onto an altar, lest your nakedness be exposed on it" (Exod 20:26). Adam and Eve found themselves needing to be clothed, the simile being: since sin had found them they needed to be covered because they were undone. We are obligated to come before God covered: our sins shame us. If we are found in public without clothes we feel ashamed and likewise if sinful humans try to enter God's presence without covering they will find themselves not only ashamed but also barred. The blood of Christ covers us, "when I see the blood, I will pass over you" (Exod 12:13). "We have confidence to enter the Most Holy Place by the blood of Jesus" (Heb 10:19).

Chapter 21 through to chapter 23:19 of Exodus contains a collection of rules that would help guide the appointed judges and people when making judicial decisions. These regulations were not the Ten Commandments but they did help implement the Ten Commandments for the conditions the Israelites were in. Each society must have laws pertaining to the circumstances they find themselves in. Later on when the nation's circumstances change, the regulations change too. That's why we have leaders who amend laws accordingly. Holding on to laws from a bygone era can damage society. Jesus was asked why Moses permitted men to divorce their wives? Jesus explained that at that time it suited the situation because men's hearts were hard, so Moses allowed it, perhaps because the alternative would be worse still. However, Christ taught us that the time to amend that law had come. A similar scenario would be that of slaves. These days having a slave is unacceptable but slavery was commonplace in the days of Moses. Time, and God's kingdom, worked towards eradicating slavery, man was told to have dominion over the animals, not other men. But at the time of the exodus, rules were needed that fit the status quo.

The last verse of this section of rulings, Exodus 23:19, informs the people not to cook a young goat in its mother's milk. Rabbinic commentators in the past suggested that the law referred to a specific foreign religious practice, in which young goats were cooked in their own mothers' milk, aiming to obtain the blessings of the gods to increase the yield of their flocks. More recently an ancient text called "the birth of the gracious gods" has been found in Ugarit. The text has been translated as saying that a ritual to ensure agricultural fertility involved the cooking of a young goat in its mother's milk, followed by the mixture being sprinkled upon the fields; although, not everyone agrees on the translation of the text. But for us and our study of the book of Exodus, we can see that the rule about the young goat did mean something to those leaving Egypt, and the chance of "the cooking of a young goat" having something to do with a blessing from the gods is strong. Particularly as the same verse that mentions the cooking of the young goat also mentions the bringing in of the first fruits. So the link between a bountiful harvest and the cooking of a young goat as some sort of sacrifice seems to be there. The point we can take from this particular "young goat" ruling is that some of these laws belonged to the time in which they were written. These days if we go into a restaurant and eat goat meat cooked in milk we do not feel obliged to enquire if the milk was from the goat's mother. The Ten Commandments stand firm, written in stone, but the rulings surrounding them alter with time and circumstance.

Critics of the book of Exodus sometimes remark that the laws we read about were not new. We must agree; they were not new. In fact, according to the book of Genesis, we have known right from wrong as part of the package of being made in God's image. The law is written on our hearts, as it is written on God's heart. The Decalogue is referred to as the "Ten Words," and Christ who came among us is introduced by John as "The Word." The Greek word John used in his Gospel is *logos*, which in Latin is *logus*, and *deca* meaning ten, gives us the word Decalogue. God's law is so close to Christ that he is named the Word. We can see Psalm 119:11 in Christ's life:

> I have hidden your word in my heart
> > that I might not sin against you.

Humanity may know right from wrong but for each human being to heed their conscience is another matter.

When I was a young boy I was taught a lesson that has stayed with me. A teacher suggested that we imagine our conscience as a triangular shape located deep within our frame. When we are tempted to do or say something that is wrong the triangle will start to spin, the sharp angles of the rotating triangle will hurt us, alerting us to the fact that we ought not to choose a particular course of action. If we listen to our conscience the triangle will stop spinning almost immediately and the discomfort will cease. If we ignore the rotating triangle, the discomfort will not stop, at least not initially. If, on proceeding occasions we continue to ignore the revolving triangle, the points of the triangle will gradually grind down because of all the friction the spinning caused and they will become less sharp and eventually become quite blunt. Thus a human being's conscience may be in a state of disrepair. In an effort to encourage new growth within the conscience, basic laws on how to behave are written down. Paul told the Romans that "when Gentiles, who do not have the law, do by nature things required by the law, they show that the requirements of the law are written on their hearts" (Rom 2:14–15). If our conscience is working well, we find that we please God by obeying the law written on our hearts, which is where God prefers the law to be written in the first place: "I will put my law in their minds and write it on their hearts" (Jer 31:33).

God knows how much light each one of us has. If we obey the light that we've been given, we'll find that more is given. "Whoever can be trusted with very little can also be trusted with much" (Luke 16:10). "Because you have been trustworthy in a very small matter, take charge of ten cities" (Luke 19:17). If the light we have is small then it can be encouraged to glow brighter when we are faced with laws that we see written down.

Some of the earliest literature ever found comes from Mesopotamia and is dated to the early 3rd millennium BC. One of these pieces, "The Instructions of Shuruppag," is written in the form of advice to the Flood hero Utnapishtim (also known as Ziusudra, and Atra-Hasis, and in the Bible as Noah) from his father. In the Bible we know the father of Noah to be Lamech (not to be confused with Lamech who descended from Cain's line). We also know that Lamech showed some wisdom and insight when he named his son Noah by using what may be a rhyming couplet: "He will comfort us in the labor and painful toil of our hands caused by the ground the Lord has cursed" (Gen 5:29). So we can see that Lamech was a man with some insight. The guidelines that were written from father to son in "The Instructions of Shuruppag" include:

"You should not speak improperly; later it will lay a trap for you."

"The eyes of the slanderer always move around as shiftily as a spindle. You should never remain in his presence."

"You should not loiter about where there is a quarrel."

And some useful practical advice:

"You should not place your house next to a public square: there is always a crowd hanging around."

Among these ancient instructions we also find:

"You should not steal."

We also find the same instruction given in the Ten Commandments. We do not find "Do not commit adultery" among "The Instructions of Shuruppag," but we do find an instruction that gets to the heart of the temptation that might cause a man to commit adultery:

"You should not sit alone in a room with a married woman."[1]

Where did Lamech get such wisdom? We may be helped in answering that question by remembering that prior to the deluge, and for some

---

1. Black et al, "Shuruppag." Note that some sources use the alternate spelling Shuruppak.

time afterwards, Yahweh was active in southern Mesopotamia. Lamech was a direct descendent of Adam—Deuteronomy 32:8 (LXX) informs us that when the Most High, "separated the sons of Adam, he set the bounds of the nations according to the number of the angels of God." Each angel watched over a nation or what we now call a Mesopotamian city-state, which seems to be why the early Sumerians had such a strong tradition of each city having its own god. Sumer never seemed to be one big nation but rather a federation of city-states, each with its own leader. The angels who resided on earth also appear to have obtained their title of "the watchers" because of this situation. It was these angels who should have been "looking out for" and "leading" the small nations or city-states of the protracted family of Adam. But rather than doing the work they had been assigned, they saw that the daughters of men (Adam) were beautiful, and took to themselves wives of all whom they chose (Gen 6:2).

Yahweh himself was looking after the direct route that would lead to his Son being born. Lamech, son of Methuselah, had a grandfather, Enoch, who walked with God. So we know from Scripture that there were some very close ties to Yahweh in the family. They learned their wisdom from the Lord and passed it down the family line.

Earlier we said that one of the oldest books in the Bible is called Job.[2] We read in the 1st and 2nd chapters what could be an annual meeting of these angels where each angel had a chance to report how events were going with their particular city-state: "on the day when God's sons came to present themselves before Yahweh" (Job 1:6 web).

Job was from the "east," which can refer to southern Mesopotamia, similar to when "the LORD God had planted a garden in the east." Or when Abraham is mentioned as originally being "one from the east" in Isaiah 41:2. A few verses later the Lord refers to Abraham as "my friend." Abraham's friendship with Yahweh began in the city of Ur. Job lived in Uz, we don't know exactly where Uz was located, but neither do we know where Akkad was located and yet we know it was an important city in Mesopotamia. According to the Dead Sea document, The War Scroll, the land of Uz is mentioned as existing somewhere beyond the Euphrates, which of course is

---

2. No scholarly consensus exists on a date for the writing of Job. The Mesopotamian region does have ancient writings, including the *Ludlul-Bel-Nimeqi* dating to around 1700 BC, that depict a good man suffering. And there is another text of earlier origin called *A Man and His God,* which was composed around 2000 BC. The book of Job offers the Christian a definitive account of a good man suffering in ancient times that occurred somewhere in the "east."

Mesopotamia. The information we have in the Bible lends itself to the possibility that when the angels came to present themselves before Yahweh (in the book of Job), the event happened on earth and not in heaven as some have supposed. If the meeting took place in heaven we are left wondering which human was also in heaven to record the event and write it down in the book of Job. But if these assemblies of the "sons of God" before Yahweh took place on earth, a man could have witnessed the meeting and took the minutes, so to speak. The local population could have known about these "meetings," some of whom may have been invited guests and able to record the proceedings. The angels would need to give an account of how their "watching" over their respective branches of Adam's family were going.

We find that Satan was also present at these meetings, but Satan is not in the same grouping as the sons of God and is not given the same title as them. He is mentioned as apart from the sons of God, probably because he was no longer considered an angel of the Lord and that he had also lost his licence to appear in the material universe. The Lord, who appears to have given Satan special dispensation to appear on earth for the duration of the meeting, detected his presence. God had reasons for allowing this dispensation, one of which could have been the recording of the conversation. The writer of the book of Job heard the discourse between the Lord and Satan, and then made his way to where Job lived because he now knew that Job was central to the story, so he was able to record the subsequent conversations between Job and his friends.

Chapter 28

Dancing For Hathor

THE MOVEMENT OF PEOPLE from Egypt to Canaan in the Exodus story seems to have a secondary strand to it. There appears to be something else "going on." The main objective is to establish the young nation of Israel in a tract of land they can call their own country, somewhere that the promised "seed" can be born. But the secondary story can trace its origins back to the rise of the Nephilim. A disturbance in the DNA genome of humanity had been creeping its way forward. Yahweh was keen to restore the natural order.

The children of Lot and his older daughter, known as the Moabites, had a part to play in the eradication of the "strange flesh." The Israelites were specifically told not to harass the Moabites because they had removed the Emites—a people strong and numerous, and as tall as the Anakites—from the land the Moabites were occupying (Deut 2:9–10). The children of Lot and his younger daughter, also played a part—the Ammonites who descended from Lot and his younger daughter's son, Ben Ammi were also protected from the Israelites' conquest when the Lord instructed the Israelites not to harass the Ammonites who had destroyed the Raphaites, a people also strong and numerous, and as tall as the Anakites (Deut 2:19–21).

The Flood had removed most of the hybrid giants but Genesis 6:4 informs us that some would survive, probably making good their escape by following the normal Fertile Crescent trade routes. It appears that a few ended up in Canaan and the surrounding area where they began to repopulate. God had people in place such as the Moabites and Ammonites to destroy them.

He also had the Israelites, and this could give us the reason why the Israelites received, what seems to us, the severe directive to destroy with the sword every living thing in Jericho—men and women, young and old.

The Israelites slowly worked their way through the land, until we read in Joshua 11:22: "No Anakites were left in Israelite territory; only in Gaza, Gath and Ashdod did any survive." And still the work of removing the unplanned DNA continued. We know that one particular giant came from Gath, whom a young Israelite from the tribe of Judah killed in the famous battle of David and Goliath.

King Og, whom Moses helped defeat, had an iron bed that measured 9 cubits long and 4 cubits wide. The bed was still a tourist attraction at the time Deuteronomy was written. Og's name could also be the origin of the modern word oger.

Once Moses has received the commands and the rulings that will help the fledgling nation of Israel run smoothly as a nation, the Lord moves on to the matter of occupying the land of Canaan (Exod 23:20). Help will be forthcoming from an angel who will work towards clearing the way for the children of Israel to settle in the land that was currently being occupied by people, some of whom, the Lord wanted removed. Joshua met the angel shortly before the battle of Jericho:

> Now when Joshua was near Jericho, he looked up and saw a man standing in front of him with a drawn sword in his hand. Joshua went up to him and asked, "Are you for us or for our enemies?" "Neither," he replied, "but as commander of the army of the LORD I have now come." Then Joshua fell facedown to the ground in reverence, and asked him, "What message does my Lord have for his servant?" (Josh 5:13–14)

The people group occupying the land would not necessarily be totally exterminated, but would lose their national identity. The Jebusites, Hittites, and others continued to inhabit Canaan, and were probably eventually immersed into the Hebrew population, having become proselytes. Provision was made for individuals and families who left the idols of their fellow compatriots and wanted to join the company of the LORD:

> The foreigner residing among you must be treated as your native-born. Love them as yourself, for you were foreigners in Egypt. (Lev 19:34)

A foreigner residing among you is also to celebrate the LORD's
Passover in accordance with its rules and regulations. You must
have the same regulations for both the foreigner and the native-
born. (Num 9:14)

As Exodus chapter 24 begins, Moses is asked by the Lord to make his
way up the mountain with over 70 prominent Israelites—a scary prospect
for those designated for the climb, as the people had not yet recovered from
the trauma of hearing the voice of God. The climbers would not only hear
God speak but also see him and eat and drink together in his presence.
Yet far from realizing their fears, they found they were not in any peril but
were rather refreshed, comforted, and filled with joy at Yahweh's resplen-
dent appearance. This close fellowship was made accessible by means of a
ceremony performed by Moses prior to the climb, where the blood of bulls
was sprinkled on the people, reflecting the blood of Christ that would one
day be shed allowing us all access into the immediate presence of God.

Moses and the men who had spent time with God on the mountain,
who had been privileged to glimpse through the backdrop of our physical dimensions, and had seen the crystal clear pavement on which Yahweh
walked, now made their way back down the mountain.

The Lord spoke again to Moses, inviting him to scale the mountain
once more and spend some time with him. The Lord also mentioned tablets
of stone. Normally, Moses did the writing, but on this occasion the Lord
said he himself had written on the tablets of stone. The relatively new alphabet-based writing would now be useful to convey God's thoughts onto a
small surface space. So Moses set out with his young protégé Joshua, whom
we suppose had the necessary permission from Yahweh to be there too.
Aaron and Hur were charged by Moses to take care of any disputes among
the people while he was on the mountain.

Moses and Joshua made their way halfway up the mountain when the
cloud covered the top of it. For six days they found themselves close to the
edges of the divine cloud. Biological life is subordinate to spirit and can be
likened to a "shadow" of true reality. The duo found themselves close to
the effervescent fountain of life, they could feel the moisture of the celestial
cloud. Their bodies no longer needing to imbibe out-sourced sustenance
because all they needed for life was there. Moses mentions the fact that he
did not need to eat or drink (Exod 34:28). He was also able to remark that
the words the people had heard were "not just idle words for you—they are
your life" (Deut 32:47).

After 6 days of enjoying the life-sustaining sublime serenity of being so close to the cloud, God called to Moses from within the cloud. Moses had tasted the heavenly tranquillity but now there was work to be done, so he entered the cloud where God could relay the plan of action that needed to be undertaken. Exodus chapters 25–31 relate what the plan of action would be: anyone whose heart was moved could make a donation of certain materials, which would then be used to make a sanctuary where God would dwell among the Israelites. The enslaved Israelites had seen magnificent structures for the worship of the Egyptian gods. They were now to have their own structure, their own "house of God." But unlike the stone-chiseled masonry of the Egyptian temples, the Israelites' construction was to be in keeping with their condition—a "tent-temple"—constructed from quality materials, which is elaborately described in six consecutive chapters.

"I will dwell among them" (Exod 25:8), were the words God spoke to Moses. The tent that was to be constructed has many parallels to Christ who also dwelt among us. In John 1:14 (kjv) where we are told that "the Word was made flesh, and dwelt among us" the Greek word for dwelt means "to have one's tent," "to dwell."

Meanwhile, back on the ground, the people had been getting restless. The people were not prepared for the 40-day-long length of time Moses was taking on the mountain with God. Patience was not one of their strong points. They piled the pressure upon Aaron and contemptuously referred to Moses as "this fellow Moses." Aaron was probably worried that the people would riot on his watch and so decided to go along with their wishes of making a god. Then, thought the people, we can get out of this wilderness. We learn from Exodus chapter 32:25 that the people of the exodus were becoming a laughingstock to their enemies, which informs us there were people nearby who could see and laugh as law and order began to break down among the exodus group. The people watching were most likely Egyptians who were now working on their next mining expedition located at the next mountain, what we know as Serabit el-Khadim.

A modern tourist attraction on Serabit el-Khadim is the ancient temple of the cow goddess Hathor. Aaron asked the people to remove their gold earrings, probably the same gold ornaments that the Egyptians had recently given them. He then appears to have rented a mold from the nearby Egyptian miners, who would also have the necessary furnace, ladles, and casting equipment. Hathor was the patron goddess of miners, which is why they built her temple so close to the mine. These proceedings would cause some laughter among the Egyptians who were aware that a God called Yahweh was supposed to be looking after the Israelites, but they now needed to borrow the goddess Hathor because it looks like Yahweh is unable to complete the task he had started. The mold obtained by Aaron would be in the shape of a cow, but Aaron would not want an exact copy of Hathor. He needed to somehow give the casted object its own identity, and so we read that after the casting Aaron "fashioned it with a tool." The engraving tool, a file of some sort, was also among the equipment rented from the Egyptians. Aaron called his finished product a calf.

We find ourselves asking the question: why did Aaron cast the shape of a calf when he had recently ate and drank in the presence of Yahweh and had seen God? The answer has two parts, firstly he cast the calf because although he had seen Yahweh, the people had not, and they were familiar with gods that looked like animals or part-animal part-human so the people would be appeased and the immediate crisis of discontent and a possible riot among the people would be averted. Secondly Aaron had found the LORD to be most welcoming, loving, kind, and gracious, so he may have thought, *I know this isn't a correct depiction of what God looks like, but I'm sure God will understand my motives.*

Aaron, the leader and an example to the people, had broken the 2nd commandment: making God's word appear cheap. Yahweh told Moses, while they were still on the mountain, that the people below them had cast an idol and were bowing down to it. Yahweh's friendship with Moses had grown close, similar to the closeness Yahweh had with Abraham. Yahweh pleads with Moses to "let Me alone, that My anger may burn against them" (Exod 32:10 nasb). The beginnings of a plague had already started to brew among the Israelites. But Moses will not let Yahweh alone and entreats him, making a case for the Israelites. The LORD even offered to make Moses into a great nation instead, which theoretically was possible, even considering the promised seed, which was working its way through the tribe of Judah. The life of long years were quickly fading for Adam's offspring but Moses still had some length of years from Adam's line, revealing that his genetic structure was robust, and Christ needed to be born of stable physical stock, without blemish, to make the perfect sacrifice. But Moses lay down his own elevation to intercede for the people he had led out of Egypt. We do not know the exact plague that God had planned for the group of people at the base of the mountain but we do know that Moses's arbitration worked and God did not bring on the people the great disaster he had threatened.

Moses started to make his downhill journey with Joshua and the two inscribed tablets, probably in Proto-Sinaitic script, written by the finger of God. During the descent Joshua remarked to Moses about the noise coming from the camp, and Moses knew what the sound was. When he reached the base of the mountain, his anger, which we have seen before, flared up with force: he threw the tablets with some strength, breaking them into pieces at the foot of the mountain. People have searched for the broken pieces of the tablets, and although fragments of rock containing Proto-Sinaitic script have been found around Serabit el-Khadim, none of them equate to the tablets that God's finger wrote upon. The broken tablets may yet be found but not at Serabit el-Khadim, they would be further along at the base of the next mountain and as far as I'm aware not too many people have looked there. Perhaps because tradition and speculation have placed Mount Sinai at a number of locations, and archaeological expeditions take time, money, and effort to arrange. We also ought to remember that over 3,400 years have passed and so sand, weather, subsidence, and settlement could have all buried the fragments deep.

The people of the exodus were out of control, to the amusement of the nearby Egyptian mineworkers. Moses asked Aaron to give an account of his actions. Aaron resorts to weak subterfuge, explaining that the gold he was given was placed into the fire and "out came this calf" (Exod 32:24). Moses was used to some supernatural experiences by this time and Aaron must have been hoping that Moses would accept his version of events. But Moses was no fool and knew that Aaron was a deft hand with smelting, casting, and the basic metallurgy of the day.

Moses looked around and saw that the rabble among the people was, as the King James Bible puts it, "naked." Which would also be an occasion for the local mineworkers to have a good laugh at Moses's and the Israelites' expense. We can assume that when Aaron made his way the few miles to the mining works in order to rent the casting equipment, a group of men went with him, some of whom may have used gold to purchase wine and beer from the mine's food service personnel. The "rabble" among them had not had any alcohol since the beginning of their journey out of Egypt, and imbibed the sudden supply of drink, which goes some way to explaining their delinquent behavior. Moses melted the calf and ground down the remains and scattered the gold dust onto the water supply, and then said, "Drink this!" and "made the Israelites drink it" (Exod 32:20).

Tough leadership was now required and Moses who had been involved in government from his earliest years took the reins back from Aaron and called for all who were on Yahweh's side to gather to him. His own tribe—the Levites—responded. Orders were then issued to cut off those involved in idolatry. They were to go through the whole camp from end to end, visit all parts of it, and wherever they saw the idolatrous rites continuing, they were to smite with the sword, and spare not.

Around 3,000 people lost their lives that day. The Levites probably had little resistance—part of the story of the Egyptian goddess Hathor was that she drank beer and became drunk and slept for three days. If the worshippers of the golden calf followed her example, the stupor of the calf worshippers would render them incapable of any realistic counteroffensive fighting. Ritual drunkenness or holy intoxication was a part of certain festivals in ancient Egypt. Hathor was sometimes known as the mistress of drunkenness. Intoxication can lower a person's ability to show restraint when it comes to sexual temptation, and in that light we understand what the King James Bible means when we read, "the people sat down to eat and to drink, and rose up to play" (Exod 32:6). The Levites would have little trouble identifying the idolaters.

Earlier we spoke about the Semitic consonants "lp" having different meanings when referring to numbers. Each time "lp" is used needs to be considered on its own merits: there could well have been 3,000 people who died, especially if we include the plague that was sent upon idolatrous offenders by the Lord (Exod 32:35).

Chapter 29

Back On Track

THE GOLDEN CALF INCIDENT had been a blow for all concerned, and was not to be taken lightly. Those who worshipped idols had been dispensed with, but there would still be consequences for those who remained. After all, if there were 25,000 people in the exodus and 3,000 of them had died, tacit approval was shown by 22,000 of them. Yahweh was not happy with their unfaithful hearts and the people themselves must have felt quite dismal. The Lord issued the disconsolate directive to "Leave this place" (Exod 33:1). In other words the Lord told the people if they wanted to leave Sinai so badly they could, "Go then and let's just forget all the great plans I had in store for you all." The Lord let Moses and the people know that they could now go and take possession of the land flowing with milk and honey, but that he himself would not be going along with them. These words caused a humility to descend upon the people and they removed their ornaments in quiet, sad contemplation. Their questioning thoughts must have been: *What about the law? Can Moses do anything to retrieve the situation? Is that it? Is our relationship with Yahweh over?* The Lord responded by saying he would "decide what to do," thereby giving the humbled people some slight hope.

The tent-temple, often referred to as the tabernacle, was yet to be constructed. Doubt now arose over the whole idea of a tabernacle. There seemed little point in its construction now that Yahweh had informed the people he would not be making the journey with them. Moses had a temporary tent of meeting, and on special occasions Moses would go to the tent, which was situated some distance from the main camp, and the pillar of cloud would descend from the heights of the mountain and stay at the entrance to this tent. Moses would speak to Yahweh face to face, as a man speaks to his friend, for by now Moses and Yahweh were good friends. They had been through a lot together, and sharing common adversity always helps to cement a friendship.

Previously, in Exodus 23:20–23, in an effort to bolster the strength of the people with some additional help, the Lord had promised to send an angel ahead of the people and Yahweh's "name is in him." The people were to listen to what the angel told them. Certain individuals among the Israelites, or their predecessors, may have already had some experience of angels. This is intimated to us because parts of the planned architecture of the tabernacle contained decorative cherubim, so those chosen to build the tabernacle must have had the knowledge of what cherubim looked like. But since the golden calf incident and the Lord's reaction of not travelling with such "stiff-necked people," the angel of high standing now seems to have been exchanged for an angel of regular standing: we do not read that this angel has the "Name" in him (Exod 32:34). We see that the Lord will keep his promise to Abraham and make sure his offspring will inherit the land promised to them, but Yahweh will not be making the journey with them. This period was a low point for the people of the exodus, the love relationship they were in with Yahweh, had suffered a serious setback, similar to a low point in the relationship between a husband and wife, or a boyfriend and girlfriend. The love affair Yahweh had with the Israelites was at an all-time low.

Moses, as Abraham before him, spoke freely to the LORD. Moses wanted to know why the Lord could not travel with the people; after all, Moses had been assigned by the Lord to the task of leading the people on their journey. Moses stood in the gap and strongly interceded on behalf of the people. The fact was, they didn't want their relationship with Yahweh to end, as we see in Exodus 33:12–17 and Exodus 34:9: "You have not let me know whom you will send with me," said Moses. "Oh Lord, if I have found favour in your eyes, then let the Lord go with us. . . . Remember that this nation is your people." Moses strongly entreated the LORD to reconsider. The humility of the people and the intercession of their advocate Moses proved effective. The LORD replied, "My presence will go with you." Moses then said, "If your presence does not go with us, do not send us up from here." "I will do what you ask," said the LORD.

Once that issue had been settled Moses asked for a special request. He had been able to converse with Yahweh face to face, as a number of people before him had. Not unlike Christ who spoke and walked among people in a normal everyday manner. Yet there was a time when Peter, James, and John were permitted to see a glimpse of Christ's glory, and Jesus was transfigured before them. Moses requests the same privilege: he asks to see a glimpse of Yahweh's glory. This event happened outside of the tent of meeting, probably on Mount Sinai. The Lord agrees to show Moses some of his glory but not all of it, Moses's human frame could not withstand the full glory, and even with a small showing of the glory of God there may be physical repercussions for Moses, though I doubt, even with hindsight, Moses would have it any other way.

Looking at Jabal Sāniyah, in close-up satellite view on an Internet map, clefts in the rock structure seem to be prevalent. This type of cleft was used by the Lord to protect Moses. Yahweh held out his hand in front of Moses's face while his glory radiated outwards from him, and as Yahweh turned he removed his hand from Moses's eyes and Moses saw Yahweh's glory. An interesting point is that Moses was also with Christ as he was transfigured. Moses had tasted the goodness of the Lord and was still being blessed by the goodness even at the time of Christ.

The Lord was willing to answer Moses's requests and Moses was also willing to fulfil the Lord's requests, one of which was to chisel out two new tablets that the Lord could write on. Moses broke the first two, which was a true picture of the law itself being broken, but now Moses must replace the tablets he broke in anger. The first tablets were the "work of God" (Exod 32:16); the second tablets were hewn by Moses.

As Moses stood there with the new tablets, the Lord again makes known a new aspect of his name. At the burning bush God had revealed his self-existent eternal nature, and now he reveals his heart of compassion and mercy.

> Yahweh, Yahweh, the compassionate and gracious God, slow to anger, abounding in love and faithfulness, maintaining love to thousands, and forgiving wickedness, rebellion and sin. (Exod 34:6–7)

God mentioned "thousands" because there were thousands in the camp, and he wanted to impress this feature of compassion, love, and mercy of his nature to them. They were being reconciled to God. And yet he also says, "he does not leave the guilty unpunished" (Exod 34:7). But it is not until we reach much further along the timeline that we realize it is God's Son who takes on himself the punishment of us all. "The punishment that brought us peace was on him, and by his wounds we are healed" (Isa 53:5). Yahweh also told Moses that he punishes the children and their children for the sin of the fathers to the third and fourth generation (Exod 34:7). We see God's child, Jesus, being punished for the sins of his earthly fathers before him, as well as for those who would follow him. The original parents are sometimes able to see the third and fourth generations, because a man and woman can live long enough to see their great grandchildren. God's Son, Jesus Christ, has had the sins of us all visited upon him and his death and resurrection stands good for all generations.

Another aspect of the divine name was then revealed to Moses.

> Do not worship any other god, for the LORD, whose name is Jealous, is a jealous God. (Exod 34:14)

Let's be sure that we are not here talking about the petty emotion caused by some loss of status, or an insecurity that causes one human to lord it over another for no other reason than their pride may be injured. This jealousy is a protective love that a father has for his children when he sees that some of them may go astray.

The Lord also modified the 2nd commandment which formerly was "You shall not make yourself a graven image."—Meaning to sculpt with a tool. When Aaron cast the calf, it could be that he and the people were hoping to be pardoned from breaking the spirit of this law by a loophole in the letter of the law, which had not mentioned "molded" idols, so this time the Lord enforced the ruling with the words, "Do not make cast idols" (Exod 34:17). The Lord spoke a number of other rulings and asked Moses to write them down. God himself wrote the Ten Commandments on the new stone tablets, and then Moses headed down the mountain with them.

A feature of seeing God's glory was the radiance reflecting from the person who saw the glory. Moses failed to realize this and when he reached the camp Aaron and the people were frightened by Moses's incandescent face. The life of God was upon him: he needed no food or drink while he was with Yahweh, the Reality at the center of the universe had drenched him with life, and he still dripped with the dew of heaven as he made his way towards the camp. This was a sign that God's glory was now back among them—the relationship was back on track.

Construction on the tabernacle (which was also the official tent of meeting) could now begin. The instructions given to Moses on Mount Sinai were meticulously followed. Chapters 35 to 39 of Exodus record the precision with which the construction complied with God's design. The Spirit of God had filled certain men among the people with artistic craftsmanship skills and on the 1st day of the New Year the tabernacle was in place. Almost a year had passed since the enslaved people had been set free. The cloud covered the tent of meeting, and the glory of the Lord filled the tabernacle. So intense was the glory that Moses had difficulty in entering—a heartfelt passionate display of God's willingness to be with his people.

Appendix

SOME OF THE WONDERS we read about in the book of Exodus were natural events that occurred providentially, which seems to be God's preferred way of working in our lives. But there were occasions when supernatural means were also at work. Archaeologists sometimes wonder why there aren't an abundance of artifacts from the wilderness if 2 million people were living there for 40 years. Firstly, we have discussed the numbers of people in the exodus and found that the actual figures were probably around 20,000 to 30,000 people. Secondly, if we accept that God was working in a special way at that time, then artifacts would be slim on the ground because Deuteronomy 29:5 says,

> During the forty years that I led you through the wilderness, your clothes did not wear out, nor did the sandals on your feet.

God placed a preservation order on the clothes and footwear of the Israelites, and he fed the people with manna so the Israelites were leading a streamlined existence. There would not be a great deal of debris or waste.

Bibliography

Austrian Archaeological Institute. Tell el-Daba archaeological dig. http://www.auaris.at/html/history_en.html.

Bennett, J. W., and M. A. Klich. "Mycotoxins." *Clinical Microbiology Reviews* 16, no. 3 (July 2003) 497–516. http://www.ncbi.nlm.nih.gov/pmc/articles/PMC164220/.

Bietak, Manfred. "The Palatial Precinct at the Nile Branch (Area H)." Tell el-Daba archaeological dig. http://www.auaris.at/html/ez_helmi_en.html#2.

Bigelow, Caroline. "List of Pharaohs." http://www.musesrealm.net/egypt/pharaohlist.html.

Black, Jeremy, et al. "The Instructions of Shuruppag." In *The Electronic Text Corpus of Sumerian Literature*. Oxford: Oxford University Press, 1998. http://etcsl.orinst.ox.ac.uk/section5/tr561.htm.

Carter, Robert. "The Neolithic Origins of Seafaring in the Arabian Gulf." *Archaeology International* (October 23, 2002). DOI: http://dx.doi.org/10.5334/ai.0613.

Chesney, Francis Rawdon. *The Expedition for the Survey of the Rivers Euphrates and Tigris*. Carried on by order of the British Government in the years 1835, 1836, and 1837. Vol. 2. London: Longman, Brown, Green, and Longmans, 1850.

Dunn, Jimmy. "Tanis (San El-Hagar)." *Tour Egypt*. http://www.touregypt.net/featurestories/tanis.htm.

Eckenstein, Lina. *A History of Sinai*. London: Society for Promoting Christian Knowledge, 1921.

Ellicott's Commentary For English Readers. "Genesis 17:1" and "Exodus 6:3." http://biblehub.com/commentaries/genesis/17-1.htm.

Gannon, Megan. "Workers at Biblical Copper Mines Ate Quite Well." *Live Science* (November 25, 2014). http://www.livescience.com/48908-metalworkers-diet-biblical-mines.html.

Gardiner, Alan. *The Admonitions of an Egyptian Sage: From a Hieratic Papyrus in Leiden*. Leipzig: Germany: Georg Olms Verlag, 1969.

———. *Egypt of the Pharaohs*. London: Oxford University Press, 1964.

Grimal, Nicolas. *A History of Ancient Egypt*. Paris: Librairie Arthéme Fayard, 1988.

Hornung, Erik. "The Pharaoh." In *The Egyptians*, edited by Sergio Donadoni, translated by Robert Bianchi et al, 283–314. Chicago: University of Chicago Press, 1997. http://press.uchicago.edu/ucp/books/book/chicago/E/bo3630993.html.

Hudec, Jozef, et al. "Tell el-Retaba: Not Only a Fortress." *Aigyptos* (May 22, 2013). http://aigyptos.sk/en/domov/tell-el-retaba-not-only-a-fortress.

Hudec, Jozef, and Veronika Dubcova. "Some Discoveries of the Early New Kingdom's Architecture in Tell el-Retaba-West." Delta and Sinai Current Research, Department of Egyptian and Nubian Archaeology, Institute of Archaeology, University of Warsaw. http://www.archeo.uw.edu.pl/zalaczniki/upload1272.pdf.

Ipuwer Papyrus. "Ancient Egyptian Didactic Literature: The Admonitions of Ipuwer." http://www.reshafim.org.il/ad/egypt/texts/ipuwer.htm.

Lennox, John C. *God's Undertaker: Has Science Buried God?* Oxford: Lion Hudson, 2009.

Malm, Sara. "'If Moses Lived Today, They'd Send Drones After Him': Christian Bale's Take on Biblical Story After He Studied it for Upcoming Film." *Daily Mail* (November 26, 2014). http://www.dailymail.co.uk/news/article-2850135/If-Moses-lived-today-d-send-drones-Christian-Bale-s-biblical-story-studied-upcoming-film.html#ixzz3KIxqI72h.

Millmore, Mark. "Thutmose III the Napoleon of Ancient Egypt." http://discoveringegypt.com/ancient-egyptian-kings-queens/thutmose-iii-the-napoleon-of-ancient-egypt/.

Numerical Recipes. "Julian Day and Civil Date Calendar." http://www.nr.com/julian.html.

Partridge, Robert B. *Fighting Pharaohs: Weapons and Warfare.* Manchester, UK: Peartree, 2002.

Peters, John P. *Nippur or Explorations and Adventures on the Euphrates: The Narrative of the University of Pennsylvania Expedition to Babylonia in the years* 1888–1890. Vol. 1. New York: G. P. Putnam's Sons, 1987.

Petrovich, Doug. "Amenhotep II and the Historicity of the Exodus Pharaoh." *Associates for Biblical Research* (Feb 2010). http://www.biblearchaeology.org/post/2010/02/04/Amenhotep-II-and-the-Historicity-of-the-Exodus-Pharaoh.aspx.

Roehrig, Catharine H., ed. *Hatshepsut: From Queen to Pharaoh.* With assistance from Renee Dreyfus and Cathleen A. Keller. Metropolitan Museum of Art, Kimbell Art Museum. New Haven, CT: Yale University Press, 2005.

Rosenmüller, Ernest Friedrich Carl. *Scholia in Vetus Testamentum.* Partis Primae, Penteteuchus Annotatione. Vol. S I–III. Leipzig, Germany: Jo, Ambros, Barthii, 1822.

Sayce, A. H., trans. "Letters by Rib-Addi of Byblos." In *Records of the Past,* 1891. Series 2, vol. 5. http://www.reshafim.org.il/ad/egypt/a-rib-addi.htm.

Tyldesley, Joyce. "Hatshepsut and Tuthmosis: A Royal Feud." *BBC* (February 17, 2011). http://www.bbc.co.uk/history/ancient/egyptians/hatshepsut_01.shtml.

Vandersleyen, Claude. *L'Égypte et la vallée du Nil,* vol. 2: *De la fin de l'Ancien Empire à*[set grave accent over a] *la fin du Nouvel Empire.* Translated by Lydia Polyakova and Inna Kumpyak. Paris: Presses Universitaires de France, 1998.

White, Jon Manchip. *Everyday Life in Ancient Egypt.* New York: Dover Publications, 2011.

Wilson, Elizabeth B. "The Queen Who Would Be King." *Smithsonian* (September 2006). Updated 2009. http://www.smithsonianmag.com/history/the-queen-who-would-be-king-130328511/?no-ist.

Lightning Source UK Ltd.
Milton Keynes UK
UKOW06f2145210916

283494UK00001B/173/P